BETWEEN HELL AND REASON

BETWEEN HELL

ALBERT

Essays from the Resistance

Selected and Translated by
Alexandre de Gramont

AND REASON
CAMUS

Newspaper *Combat*, 1944–1947

Foreword by Elisabeth Young-Bruehl

WESLEYAN UNIVERSITY PRESS
Published by University Press of New England
Hanover and London

Wesleyan University Press
Published by University Press of New England, Hanover, NH 03755

English translation copyright © 1991 by Alexandre de Gramont

Foreword, copyright © 1991 by Elisabeth Young-Bruehl

All the articles by Camus were collected in French in either *Essais* © 1965, Editions Gallimard et Calmann-Lévy, or *Actuelles: I: Chroniques* © 1950 Editions Gallimard. Used by permission of Editions Gallimard and Mme Catherine Camus.

Copies of the original articles are in a number of archives but the translator has relied on the original collections of the New York Public Library.

Printed in the United States of America   5 4 3 2 1

LIBRARY OF CONGRESS CATALOGING-IN-PUBLICATION DATA

Camus, Albert, 1913–1960.
    Between hell and reason: essays from the Resistance newspaper
Combat, 1944–1947 / selected and translated by Alexandre de Gramont;
foreword by Elisabeth Young-Bruehl.—1st ed.
        p.   cm.
    Bibliography: p.
    Includes index.
    ISBN 0-8195-5188-0   ISBN 0-8195-5189-9 (pbk.)
    1. World War, 1939–1945—France. 2. World War, 1939–1945—
Underground literature—France. I. De Gramont, Alexandre, 1963–   .
II. Title
D802.F8C343   1989   87-21331
940.53'44—dc19   CIP

Heroism isn't much . . . happiness is more difficult.
—*Letters to a German Friend*

Before the terrifying prospects now available to humanity, we see even more clearly that peace is the only goal worth struggling for. This is no longer a prayer but a demand to be made by all peoples to their governments—a demand to choose definitively between hell and reason.
—*Combat*, 8 August 1945

Contents

Contents

viii

Contents

Foreword

Selections from the editorials Albert Camus wrote between 1944 and 1947 for the Resistance newspaper *Combat* have been published in the French editions of his short prose pieces, *Essais* and *Actuelles,* but no *oeuvre complet* exists. Only a few of the editorials from *Combat* have appeared in English, and they are scattered in various journals and anthologies. The selection of Camus's *Combat* pieces that Alexandre de Gramont has translated and introduced in this volume is designed both to recapture a crucial moment in French and European history recorded by an astute and passionate participant and to indicate how Camus's Resistance experience informed his later work.

Camus's wartime journalism has been overshadowed by the many editions in many languages of his novels—*The Stranger, The Plague*—his plays—*Caligula, The Possessed*—and his long philosophical essays—*The Myth of Sisyphus* and *The Rebel.* Although persons concerned with political thinking in the mid-twentieth century can readily find the texts to consider what *Homage to Catalonia* meant for George Orwell's *1984,* or what Hannah Arendt's essays on "the Jewish Question" meant for *The Origins of Totalitarianism,* they could only trace the connection between Camus's prewar work and his work after the war by a circuit into the archives of the Bibliothèque Nationale. This collection of Camus's *Combat* pieces provides the essential texts.

Camus's later work continually referred, implicitly and explicitly, to the hopefulness he had felt as the war ended: hopefulness for a new France, a new Europe, a new politics built upon the spontaneous solidarity of the Resistance and the public happiness of the Liberation. Camus's *Combat* editorials chronicle this vision—from its inception to its end. As the old France, the old Europe, the familiar politics of class struggle, party faction, and public cynicism re-emerged, he was filled with despair. But he was not content to lay blame elsewhere. There was something, he felt, in the dynamics of the Resistance itself that destroyed its possibilities.

The *Combat* editorials also chronicle Camus's self-critique and his critique of the Resistance. What came chiefly to issue was murder. He and most of his Resistance colleagues had argued that traitors to France, Nazi collaborators, Nazi murderers, deserved justice in kind—life for life—and thus the death penalty. But he saw this judgment turn into a policy of summary executions and vendettas; in the very beginning of the peace, there was a near civil war of vengeance. And from the lesson of this smaller war, Camus fashioned a tempered vision: not a "new" politics, but a politics of limits, of moderation and mediation. Like Orwell and Arendt, he turned to the unfulfilled hopes, the best wishes, of the old, Greco-Roman political tradition. By the time he wrote *The Rebel*, which was published in 1951, he was invoking, poetically, almost mystically, "our common Mediterranean heritage."

The complex weave of hope and disillusionment that Camus wrote as the post-war era began looks, from the present moment, which we judge to be the end of the post-war era, like a familiar pattern. A Cold War can also finish, we find, in a confusion of new possibilities and old spectres. Camus's *Combat* commentary could, should, strike a chord of recognition currently—as his better-known work has before.

Dwight Macdonald had introduced the readers of his journal *Politics* to the *Combat* editorials in 1947 by excerpting and translating Camus's meditation on revolutionary violence and the death penalty. Macdonald also provided to his readers translations of pieces by Simone Weil, who appealed to the same desire for a humane, unorthodox socialism. But not until students at Berkeley and Chicago and Columbia shared around worn, much-discussed copies of *The Rebel* in the late 1960s did Camus's quest for political morality have a broad American echo. He was read then as a theorist who had struggled to understand why and how revolutionaries so often turn to excesses of violence, producing variations of the tyrannies and the authoritarian regimes they had set out to overthrow. Camus's impassioned advocacy of moderation in political theory and practice, and his invocation of the spirit of political solidarity, were received by the like-minded 1960s American rebels as cautionary tales for the Left. Fascism seemed to them a kind of contagious disease, an epidemic that had surfaced in the "Establishment" that supported the war in Vietnam but threatened to make its way into the ranks of the anti-establishmentarians. In Camus's book, as in those of Orwell and Arendt, they found the antidote: republicanism and critique of all ideologies aspiring to totalism.

As a warning to revolutionaries of the Left Camus's work has few equals. But it is not the historical process by which rebellion turns into revolution and revolution into terror that is on the minds of those on the current American Left. They have had to work mightily to generate even a little domestic rebellion against leaders who, while celebrating the bicentennial of the transition from revolution to Constitution, have been incapable of understanding revolutionary hopes, at home or elsewhere. Camus's warning would seem more immediately to apply to events abroad: most specifically to the countries in Eastern Europe as they struggle for democracy and humane socialism after forty years of Soviet "colonialism," and more variously to the lands that make up the vast preponderance of the planet, but are called by us, condescendingly, "the Third World." Rebellions and revolutions so variegated that they have strained to the breaking point the midcentury European denominations "from the Left" and "from the Right" are in process on every continent; each one has its own debates over the dilemmas of violence, as each one has its Camus-like voices of hard-learned restraint.

When Camus was writing his *Combat* editorials, he realized that the world after the war would be as intranationally linked as the war itself had been. No more than anyone else, however, did he foresee how crucially the internal dynamics of postwar revolutions would be influenced by geopolitics, how complexly superpower imperialistic struggles would be woven into national and regional struggles. Nor did he understand until the Algerian War made it clear to him that anticolonialist revolutions or movements for national liberation would have dynamics in many ways different from the Resistance and from the French and Russian revolutions that had given him and his contemporaries their sense of precedents.

But it is not for his historical grasp or his prescience that Camus remains an important political thinker. He is exemplary primarily for the way he thought: how he framed questions so that he, the framer of the questions, never disappeared, leaving responsibility for the questions to others; how he registered his own errors and built the principles they revealed into his next effort; how he assumed that thinking is rethinking and then always yet more rethinking, so that—as he said in *The Rebel*—"to breathe is to judge." In his novels and plays and philosophical essays, Camus's hard-working understanding is visible in public tableaux. His *Combat* editorials are a workshop, a place where moral didacticism and homily are mixed with query and call to reconsideration, where utopianism struggles against fatigue at the hard realities, where both the high-flying rhetoric of the barricades and the hard-hitting rhetoric of ideology-critique were tethered by tragic lament.

> Elisabeth Young-Bruehl
> *Wesleyan University*
> *December 1990*

Preface and Acknowledgments

In the summer of 1985 when I was searching for a project for my undergraduate thesis at Wesleyan University, I discovered that Albert Camus's writings for the French Resistance newspaper *Combat* had never been translated into English. The idea of translating Camus's *Combat* writings immediately attracted me for several reasons: I had read and loved Camus's novels, plays, and essays; I had always been interested in that period of history for my grandfather fought and died in the French Resistance; I liked the challenge of translating never-before-translated material.

I knew little about the *Combat* writings when I first began to read them, and what I found surprised me: Camus, whom I admired for his moderation and his opposition to the death penalty, advocated a purge and sanctioned executions. I was fascinated that one could see in these articles Camus's gradual disillusionment with political violence, that one could trace the formation of his decision to oppose henceforth executions and all political violence—no matter what the circumstances. The *Combat* writings seemed to me to constitute a "missing link" between Camus's pre- and post-war work, to explain why Camus's major concern shifted from suicide in *The Myth of Sisyphus* to murder in *The Rebel.*

The articles presented here represent less than a third of Camus's writings for *Combat.* Camus's complete writings for *Combat* include everything from theater reviews to an indignant condemnation of the government's tax on cinema tickets, as well as articles on Franco's Spain and Algeria.

I had originally chosen for this collection only the articles that seemed most related to Camus's transition of thought from *The Myth of Sisyphus* to *The Rebel.* However, when I wrote to the Camus estate to ask for permission to publish this selection in translation, I was told that twelve of the articles I had chosen had not been definitely established as Camus's.

Actually, eleven of the twelve articles in question are accepted as Camus's by a number of scholars. One of these articles (30 December 1944), in fact, was signed. Two of them (March 1944 and May 1944) were identified by Camus himself for biographer Germaine Brée. (These two were the only articles from the underground pre-Liberation *Combat* ever to have been positively identified as Camus's—all of his other *Combat* writings are post-Liberation.) Eight of the remaining nine (21 August 1944, 22 August 1944, 4 September 1944, 6 September 1944, 6 October 1944, 18 October 1944, 2 November 1944, and 8 November 1944) were identified through the work of Roger Quilliot (editor of Camus's *Essais,* published by Gallimard) and of Professor Emmett Parker of the University of Alabama (author of perhaps the best study of Camus's journalism, *Albert Camus: The Artist in the Arena*). Both Quilliot and Parker were given access by the late Mme Albert Camus to a file of carbon copies of the articles Camus had kept. In an introductory note in *Essais,* Quilliot points out that Camus would have had no reason to keep these copies had they not been his own. Professor Parker recently told me that all of the articles in this file had been written on the same typewriter, and that all corrections were in Camus's hand. As for the twelfth article (17 August 1945), it was similar enough in content and style to convince me it was Camus's.

Definitive authentication must rest with the Camus estate, and so I have omitted these twelve articles, though I refer to them in my Introduction. I have substituted for the twelve articles other essays that are, on the whole, as good as those I have omitted, though they are not always as directly related to the evolution of Camus's thinking on revolution and violence which the collection is meant to show. (Among these added articles there is, for example, a fine essay on the tragedy of separation that was a consequence of the Occupation, which foreshadows an important theme of *The Plague*.) I trust that the evolution of his thought on revolution will be evident despite the substitutions.

It is important to remember that the *Combat* articles were written during a time when many of the French people truly believed a new beginning was possible. Many of the articles are filled with what Camus later called "the fever of those years." The result, though, is that the quality of articles is uneven. It is obvious that some were carefully planned and written (most notably those in "Neither Victims nor Executioners"), while others were written hurriedly and impatiently. The articles of the early weeks of the Liberation, especially, seem like oratory; they are filled with short, sloganlike sentences and on occasion end with a long and rather unwieldy peroration. Surely this is due in part to the circumstances of the time, and in part to the manner in which Camus prepared the early editorials: he would simply write down notes from which he would then dictate the text to a secretary— with no revisions afterward.

I have tried to retain the flavor of Camus's texts while at the same time translating them into readable English. "Neither Victims nor Executioners" was translated earlier into English in slightly excerpted form by Dwight Macdonald in *Politics*, vol. 4, no. 4 (July–August 1947), and Justin O'Brien translated four *Combat* articles (not included in this volume) in the anthology *Resistance, Rebellion and Death*. I have consulted both men's work. A number of Camus studies quote short passages of the *Combat* articles in translation, and I have on occasion consulted these as well (especially Emmett Parker's *Albert Camus: The Artist in the Arena*).

I would like to thank Prof. Norman R. Shapiro for help with some translating difficulties, and Prof. Carl A. Viggiani for all his help and encouragement. And I must express my deep gratitude to Prof. Elisabeth Young-Bruehl, who went painstakingly through nearly all the French and translated texts, as well as through several versions of the translator's introduction, always making helpful changes, suggestions, and corrections.

Alexandre de Gramont
Lawrenceville, N.J.
January 1991

TRANSLATOR'S INTRODUCTION

I.

The Resistance newspaper *Combat* first appeared openly on the streets of liberated Paris in late August 1944. Its editor-in-chief was the young philosopher and novelist Albert Camus. Beginning in the final year of the Occupation and continuing for several years after the Liberation, Camus wrote close to a hundred and fifty articles and editorials for *Combat*. A selection of those writings is presented here for the first time in English.

Combat the newspaper began as part of the Combat Resistance network, whose origins can be traced to the beginnings of the French Resistance. Germany had invaded France in May 1940 and France had fallen one month later. The French parliament had turned over near-monarchical powers to Marshal Philippe Pétain who, along with Pierre Laval, negotiated an armistice with Germany that created a "free" French zone south of the Loire with its capital in Vichy. The north of France, including Paris, was occupied by the Germans.

In the summer of 1940 Henri Frenay, a French army officer captured by the Germans, escaped, crossed into the Vichy Zone, and began to organize a small Resistance network. Most early resistance began in the form of small underground newspapers, and the activities of Frenay's group were at first confined to pub-

3

lication of a news sheet which shared the name of the network, Les Petites Ailes de la France (The Little Wings of France). But Frenay was determined to make his group a military organization as well. He soon changed the name of the network and the newspaper to Combat, and had his group carrying out missions of intelligence-gathering and sabotage in addition to writing, printing, and distributing the underground paper.

The first issue of the newspaper bearing the name *Combat* had appeared in December 1941.[1] The articles and editorials of *Combat* and the other clandestine papers were devoted primarily to reports of Nazi atrocities, correction of news printed in the collaborationist press, condemnation of the Vichy government, and messages from Charles de Gaulle, leader of the government-in-exile in England.[2] In 1942 Combat's paper appeared sporadically with a circulation of about 30,000. (By "circulation" is meant the number of issues printed; the actual readership was probably much higher since the papers were passed from one person to another.[3]) By 1943 *Combat* appeared once or twice a month with a circulation of 120,000, and by 1944 the figure was over 200,000.

After the Liberation, *Combat* became the talk of Paris. Everybody who was anybody read *Combat*.[4] Its contributors included André Gide, Jean-Paul Sartre, Simone de Beauvoir, André Breton, and Denis de Rougement. *Combat* was filled with the excitement and exhilaration of Paris in the post-Liberation days. Camus wrote in his editorials of a new French society that would be built out of the Resistance forces. He demanded wide-ranging social and economic change, and a political system based on the moral principles that had united the Resistance.

During the winter of 1944–45, however, it became increasingly clear that the dream of a Resistance-based society emerging in post-Liberation France would not be realized. The Resistance began to splinter into more or less the same ideological factions that had existed before the war. Nor could the enormous success of Camus's *Combat* last without the spirit of Resistance unity. The staff of *Combat* began to differ on fundamental ideological issues; Sartre and the young leftists sympathized with the Communist and Socialist parties, while others turned toward the Gaullists. Camus was isolated somewhere between the two extremes. Starting in January 1945, Camus took increasingly longer leaves of absence from *Combat* to work on his own writings. Sartre soon left with his followers to start the monthly journal *Les Temps modernes.*

By 1947, when *Combat*'s readership had already diminished considerably, a month-long printers' strike crippled the paper financially. *Combat* was sold to Henri Smadja, a Tunisian businessman with Socialist leanings. Camus announced his resignation from *Combat* on 3 June 1947. Claude Bourdet, one of the original leaders of the Combat movement, took his place as editor-in-chief. *Combat* would continue to be published under various editors until 1974, but never with anything like the success of the post-Liberation months.

II.

Albert Camus was among the least systematic of thinkers. The evolution of his thought was rarely a logical or highly cerebral process. Rather, his ideas developed according to his visceral reactions to his experiences and observations. This is why Camus's journalism, in which he recorded and commented on what he believed to be the most important events of his day, provides so many insights into the rest of his work. The *Combat* writings, especially, both in the events they discuss and the hopes and aspirations they reveal, represent an extremely important phase in the development of Camus's thinking.

Camus's major works written before his participation in the Resistance, particularly *The Myth of Sisyphus,* were characterized by moral solipsism and a world view that could reasonably be construed, and often has been, as nihilistic. In *The Myth of Sisyphus*, completed at the beginning of 1941, Camus wrote of a metaphysical revolt (also translated into English as "rebellion") against the meaninglessness of the world. He urged people to protest this meaninglessness and their ultimate fate, death, by leading lives as full as possible, unlimited by moral codes or other restrictions. The quantity rather than the quality of experience was what counted.

But after 1942, in France under the Occupation, Camus's ideas about revolt began to change drastically. The nature of the struggle against the Nazis, the utter brutality the members of the Resistance faced, led Camus to believe that true revolt protested not only the world's lack of meaning but the world's lack of justice as well. Revolt became an assertion of moral values.

In the months immediately following the Liberation, Camus believed, the Resistance fighters could continue their moral rebellion, and indeed turn it into a moral revolution that would bring significant reform to France and perhaps even to the rest of Europe. As part of the revolution Camus, who would later be renowned for his impassioned rejection of political violence and the death sentence, advocated a purge of the old political order—a purge that included executions of collaborators and traitors. As the purge rapidly deteriorated into a series of personal vendettas and summary executions, Camus realized that his hopes for meaningful social and political reform would not be fulfilled.

The *Combat* writings chronicle Camus's call to revolution, his support of the purge, his hopes for the new society he thought would emerge, his gradual disillusionment with the "revolution," and his growing realization that France would not be significantly changed by the forces of the Resistance. By the time he was writing his last articles for *Combat*, he had come to the conclusions for which he is now famous: that he would henceforth oppose all political violence (including the death penalty) and instead advocate moderation, caution, and recognition of human limitations. Violence and revolution were no longer legitimate consequences of revolt. Though violence is sometimes necessary to defend oneself (as it was during the Occupation), violence can never be legitimized (as it was during the Liberation). Human life must be asserted before all other values. Camus would put forth these conclusions in more elaborate form several years later in *The Rebel* of 1951.

One critic writes that during the years of Occupation and post-Liberation, Camus's primary concern shifted from "the situation of the lone individual to that of the community."[5] This is not entirely accurate. Camus's concern shifted, but not so much to the community at large as to the problems of the individual committed to serving that community. Camus himself always felt a strong sense of responsibility toward his fellow human being and toward improving the conditions of society. Yet as Susan Tarrow writes, his sense of personal commitment "did not resolve the problems involved in finding acceptable channels for that commitment."[6] Except when he was writing for *Combat*, Camus had little faith that the collective endeavor of politics could ever be truly effective. Long before the Resistance Camus had believed, and would believe again afterward, that political goals tended to be vague and distracting, that political systems could never fully consider the needs of the average man and of the poor, that politicians were inevitably blind to what was really at stake. He had written before the war in 1938: "politicians have no idea how difficult it is simply to be a man: to live, without being unjust, a life filled with inequities, on 1,200 francs a month, with a wife, a child and the certainty of dying without being inscribed in the textbooks of history."[7]

Camus's involvement with the Resistance led him to change his mind momentarily about the possibilities of politics. He believed that the men and women who had united in the common cause of the Resistance could continue united after the war so as to change entirely the nature of politics. But after the failure of a Resistance-based society to emerge out of the Liberation, and after the disastrous purge which Camus himself had recommended to bring about such a society, he returned to his pessimistic views concerning politics.

But while Camus was left disillusioned with politics itself, the *Combat* years further convinced him of the individual's responsibility to the collectivity, and provided him, through the evolution of his theory of revolt, with rules and a rationale for commitment. Revolt had now become an affirmation of common moral values, as well as an obligation to assert those values against injustice. Yet this assertion had its limits: human life was to be respected above all. To be sure, the new form of revolt as an approach to commitment did not always prove unproblematic for Camus. In many ways, his life would always be an ongoing search for an appropriate and satisfactory means of commitment.

III.

Camus had entered the world of politics in the summer of 1935, shortly before his twenty-second birthday, when he joined the Communist Party in his native Algeria, still a French colony at that time. Camus had misgivings about communism from the beginning, but he told his teacher and mentor, Jean Grenier, that he was obliged to become a Communist in order to remain close to the people with whom he identified, the working class of Algiers, and that one could "accept activity in favor of Communism while remaining pessimistic with respect to it."[8]

Camus did well in the Party. According to one biographer, he "was an excellent Communist: zealous and tough."[9] Yet Camus disliked Communist orthodoxy, with its absolute truths and historical determinism, and he distrusted the Party leadership. His opposition to the romance of communism remained steady. In March 1936 he wrote in his notebook: "Grenier on Communism: 'The entire question is this: for the sake of an ideal of justice, must one subscribe to all sorts of nonsense?' To answer 'yes,' is beautiful; to answer 'no,' is honest." [10]

The immediate source of Camus's discontent with the Parti Communiste Algérien (P.C.A.) was its changing attitude toward the Algerian Moslems. The Communist Party had long focused its attention on the Moslems, who made up the vast majority of the Algerian population but were entirely disenfranchised under the French colonial system. The Communist Party platform had promised to promote the liberation of the colonies, and Camus later said that "recruitment in Arab circles" represented half his Party activities.[11] But when Stalin, faced with the growing threat of Nazi Germany, decided that the interests of the Soviet Union would best be served by a strong and friendly France, the French and Algerian Communist parties were told by Moscow to revise their attitudes toward French colonial policies, and toward the Algerian Moslems as well.

It took some time for the new line to make its way down to the working level.[12] But by 1937 the P.C.A.'s new attitude had become increasingly clear. Camus felt that the Communist Party had been exploiting the Moslems' misery for purely political ends and was now abandoning them out of political expediency. He protested the new Party line openly and often, and was subsequently called to Party headquarters and told to revise his position. He refused. In November 1937 the Party leadership voted to expel him.

Camus would later write Grenier that he had been "duped" by communism: "My only excuse, if I have one at all, is that I cannot detach myself from the people among whom I was born and whom I can never abandon. Communism has unfairly annexed their cause. I understand now that if I have a duty, it is to give my people the best of myself, that is, to defend them against lies." [13] Camus's experiences in the Party, and what he had seen of the French colonial government in Algeria, convinced him that politicians were either selfish and corrupt, or dedicated to overly broad and abstract goals which caused them to neglect the people they were meant to serve. He wrote in his notebook in December 1937, the month after his expulsion from the P.C.A.: "Politics and the fate of mankind are shaped by men without greatness. Those who possess greatness are not in politics." [14]

After the P.C.A., Camus never joined another political party. He did, however, join the staff of *Alger-Républicain,* an Algiers daily started in 1938 which backed the Popular Front—the coalition of left-of-center groups that had twice made Léon Blum premier of France in the late 1930s. *Alger-Républicain* was founded by Jean-Pierre Faure, a liberal French Algerian businessman who had as friends men like André Malraux and Louis Aragon. When Faure went to France to look for an editor, Aragon suggested Pascal Pia, then a news editor at *Ce Soir.* Pia agreed to come to Algeria and edit the paper.

Journalism suited Camus far better than party activism. As a journalist he could stand aside and help guide politics from an objective viewpoint. He could rally to the aid of the "average" man and the weaker members of society, so often disenfranchised by the indifference and stupidity of politicians and the greed of the privileged. Camus specialized in exposés and press campaigns on behalf of the victims of political and administrative injustice.[15] For instance, he defended Michel Hodent, a government grain agent who had been wrongly accused of defrauding Moslem farmers. After careful investigation Camus discovered that the judge, the local planters, and the *caïds*— Moslem leaders appointed by the French—were all involved in an attempt to discredit a government program to support grain prices that had been enacted under the Blum administration.[16] Camus succeeded in obtaining Hodent's release. He also defended El Okbi, a prominent Moslem spokesman who had been charged with murder for what Camus believed were political reasons.[17] El Okbi, too, was eventually released. In 1939 Camus wrote a series of eleven articles on "The Poverty of Kabylia," a region in the mountainous area between Algiers and Constantine that had been struck by terrible famine. After describing the region's suffering, and attacking the colonial policies that had given away the Moslems' best land to French settlers, he suggested wide reforms.

When England and France declared war on Germany in September 1939, Pascal Pia decided to merge *Alger-Républicain* with its afternoon paper in order to devote fuller coverage to the war. Thus was born *Soir-Républicain,* of which Camus became an editor. *Soir-Républicain*'s editorial line closely followed the pacifist point of view formulated by Léon Blum.[18] Camus believed that the European democracies were also responsible for the war and that they should do everything possible to arrive at a truce. He criticized Hitler, but argued nonetheless that Germany did have certain legitimate grievances. He thought that the war would resolve nothing, that it would be long, and that working men would be slaughtered.[19]

Camus became more and more depressed as it became apparent that a full-scale war would not be averted. He tried to enlist in the army but was turned down because he suffered from tuberculosis. He had sought to enlist, he told Grenier, not because he accepted the war, but so as not to use his illness as a shield, and also to express solidarity with those called up to fight.[20] He wrote in *Soir-Républicain* on 17 September 1939: "Never perhaps have left-wing militants had so many reasons to despair.

Many beliefs have collapsed along with this war. And amid all the contradictions that the world founders in, forced to see things clearly, we are then led to deny everything." [21]

In the following months Camus and Pia battled with military censorship. Also, they were running out of paper. Knowing that *Soir-Républicain* would eventually be closed made them even more combative and uncompromising than usual. [22] First the military authorities imposed sanctions and then in January 1940, a few days before the supply of paper was exhausted, they banned *Soir-Républicain*.

Pascal Pia returned to France, and Camus followed him several months later. Pia had found him a job at *Paris-Soir* working on layout and rewrite. He concentrated on his own writing, finishing *The Stranger* in May 1940 and continuing work on *The Myth of Sisyphus*. When France fell in 1940, *Paris-Soir* moved to Lyons and Camus went with it. But *Paris-Soir* was soon publishing a much smaller edition, requiring fewer workers. Camus lost his job and returned to Algeria. He worked for a time in a private school in Oran, where in February 1941 he completed *The Myth of Sisyphus*.

IV.

The solipsism of *The Stranger* and *The Myth of Sisyphus* is striking, when one considers Camus's history as a Communist Party member and *Alger-Républicain*'s crusading journalist. Camus's despair at the inevitability of the war, the most catastrophic consequence of human society, clearly contributed to the extremely grim outlook of his work at that time. He wrote in his notebook in March 1940:

More and more, when faced with the world of men, the only reaction is individualism. Man alone is an end unto himself. Everything you try to do for the common good ends in failure. Though you want to try nonetheless, decency demands that you do so with the required amount of scorn. Withdraw into yourself completely, and play your own game.[23]

In *The Stranger* and *The Myth of Sisyphus,* Camus addressed the problem of "the absurd," which he defined in *The Myth of Sisyphus* as the individual's "wild longing for clarity" combined with the universe's inability to provide that clarity. How is the individual who longs for meaning and clarity to act when faced with a meaningless, chaotic existence, at the end of which comes an equally meaningless death?

The main character of *The Stranger,* Meursault, is an individual clearly estranged from society; he continuously ignores society's rules not because he is rebellious but because he is oblivious. He knows and says only what he feels. More important, Meursault is estranged from existence itself. Life "appears senseless to him at every moment, not because of any intellectual reasons, but from immediate evidence."[24] Yet this estrangement does not at first cause him despair. For the most part, he lives happily, from moment to moment, from experience to experience. Only after he is condemned to death for a series of events that to him were entirely discontinuous and unrelated,[25] must Meursault come to terms with the absurd.

The novel begins when Meursault, a clerk in an Algiers office, learns by telegram that his mother has died in an old-age home outside the city. Meursault attends the funeral. The next day he goes swimming and meets Marie, a woman who once worked in his office. He takes her to a comic film and begins an affair with her that evening. Some time later Meursault and Marie are invited by Meursault's neighbor, a shady character named Raymond, to spend a weekend at the beach. There they encounter several Arabs, one of whom has a grudge against Raymond. In the confrontation that follows, Meursault shoots and kills one of the Arabs.

In the second part of the novel, Meursault is brought to trial. It becomes immediately apparent that he is being tried not so much for killing a man as for having disregarded certain norms of society: he drank *café au lait* and smoked cigarettes at his mother's wake; he failed to cry at her funeral; he began an affair the day after. This, the prosecutor says, shows that Meursault was "a criminal at heart" long before the murder. That Meursault actually did commit murder seems of secondary importance to the court. Nonetheless, he is found guilty and sentenced to execution by the guillotine. Tarrow notes that Meursault's being condemned to death for murdering an Arab in French colonial Algeria has often been criticized as unrealistic. But the point is that Meursault "is condemned not for murder, but for subverting the status quo." [26]

While awaiting execution, Meursault for the first time questions the nature of his existence. He is particularly obsessed by the overwhelming certainty of death, which so surely renders all else meaningless: "The death of others, or the love of a mother, or God—what could these things matter to me? Or the way a man decides to live his life, or the fate he thinks he chooses, when it is one fate and one fate only that chooses me." [27] It is then that he realizes that death is nothing but an invitation to live as fully and freely as possible, that within the small time span of the human life there are an infinite number of joys to be experienced. This is Meursault's moment of rebellion, as well as the rationale for the way he has lived: despite death, he has chosen happiness; when his death is imminent, he chooses happiness still.

In *The Myth of Sisyphus* Camus attempted to give a more systematic exposition of this rationale for existence. The "one truly serious philosophical problem," *The Myth of Sisyphus* proclaims, "is that of suicide." Will the individual decide that his own life is worth living? The problem arises in the face of the absurd. Because there is an inherent quality in the human individual that demands meaning from his world, and because the world fails to provide that meaning, the individual is tempted to negate one of the two elements that make up the absurd equation: either his world or himself. These two forms of negation, Camus wrote, are the traditional reactions to the absurd. In the first, one rejects one's world to choose transcendence and to put one's faith in an afterlife in which divinity will provide intelligibility. This is the leap of faith; Camus called it philosophical suicide. The second reaction, "more irremediable than the first in its consequences and hence less frequently carried out,"[28] is, of course, physical suicide: the absurd is suppressed through the death of the individual who has experienced the world's insignificance. The alternative Camus proposed is to maintain one's balance on the "dizzying crest" that lies between philosophical and physical suicide. The individual rebels against meaninglessness and this rebellion gives life its purpose and value.

The archetypical absurd hero for Camus was Sisyphus, fated for eternity to roll a boulder up a mountain, only to have it tumble back just before reaching the summit. His task seems hopeless, his situation absurd. Yet he concentrates his every effort on the rock during the climb; he devotes all his strength, mental and physical, to his attempt to reach the summit, even though he will never succeed. Each time Sisyphus descends the mountain to return to the boulder, he realizes the utter futility of his task yet takes it up again. His persistence represents his revolt against futility and makes him superior to his fate. As was the case with Meursault, the futility of the world can suppress neither Sisyphus nor his happiness. Indeed, Camus concludes, one "must imagine Sisyphus happy."

Camus wrote in *The Myth of Sisyphus* that since the individual's ultimate fate is death, proper rebellion against that fate involves living according to a quantitative rather than qualitative ethic. One must "use up everything that is given"; a wealth of experience is what counts. This "ethic of quantity" was one of the more troublesome aspects of the book, and Camus was unable to maintain it. As John Cruickshank has noted, Camus "found it impossible to retain the absurdist ethic in the face of a particular, concrete situation. A quantitative morality might have led as easily to the black market as to the Resistance—indeed it did so in many cases."[29]

Not until Camus experienced the German Occupation did he truly live and breathe the nihilism of his time.[30] In his pacifist views at the beginning of the war, Camus clearly had not understood the nature of Hitler's Germany. He had not considered in *The Myth of Sisyphus* an important consequence of the absurd, that one might commit "philosophical suicide" not in the form of religion but in the form of totalitarianism.

V.

In the summer of 1942 Camus was in Oran, suffering one of his many attacks of tuberculosis. He decided to go to France to take a cure. His wife's cousin owned a boarding house in Le Panelier, a village in the Massif Central not far from Lyons. There Camus could rest in the mountain air. He had planned to spend only a few months in Le Panelier and then return home to continue work on his writing. But in November the Allies invaded North Africa. Hitler ordered all France occupied, and Camus was cut off from his wife, mother, and friends in Algeria. "Like rats!" he wrote in his notebook.[31] There are two interpretations to this entry: either he felt trapped like a rat or, more likely, the movement of German troops reminded him of an invasion of rats—"the brown plague," as the Nazis were called.[32]

It is not clear exactly when and how Camus became involved in Resistance activities. Though he may have made contact with the Combat organization as early as that autumn of 1942, he did not begin working on *Combat* until, at the earliest, the summer of 1943. There are several versions of how he came to join the *Combat* staff.[33] The most probable is that given by the French Resistance historians Marie Granet and Henri Michel in their history of the Combat movement. According to Granet and Michel, Combat's director, Henri Frenay, had decided to move the center of Combat's operations from Lyons to Paris in August 1943. The editorial staff of *Combat* would also go to Paris, but the printing press had to remain in Lyons. Co-ordinating the work of the writers and editors in Paris with the work of the printers in Lyons would be a complex and dangerous task. Frenay asked Pascal Pia, Camus's friend and editor from *Alger-Républicain,* to be *Combat*'s editor and supervise this project. When Pia found himself too busy with other Resistance activities, he asked Camus, who by this time had moved from Le Panelier to Paris, to take his place. Camus accepted his offer.[34]

Between the time when he was cut off from Algeria and the time he joined *Combat,* Camus began to come to terms with some of the problems of the absurdist ethic in his *Letters to a German Friend.* Using the literary device of four letters written to a former comrade (the first two letters were published, respectively, in the underground newspapers *Revue libre* and *Cahiers de la libération* during the Occupation[35]), Camus describes how the absurd led the Germans and the French Resistance fighters to take very different forms of action. According to Camus's interpretation, the Germans, too, had started from recognition of the absurd. But rather than rebel against the cruelty and chaos of the universe, they decided to live according to its rules, so they deified the state to pursue the adventure of power. He wrote in the fourth letter:

You supposed that in the absence of any human or divine code the only values were those of the animal world—in other words, violence and cunning. Hence you concluded that man was negligible and that his soul could be killed, that in the maddest of histories the only pursuit for the individual was the adventure of power and his own morality, the realism of conquests.[36]

The German's brand of nihilism was like nothing Camus had anticipated in *The Myth of Sisyphus*, and their wartime atrocities led Camus to serious rethinking. Camus's rebellion began to take on new form: the human being rebels against the universe's lack of justice as well as against its lack of meaning, for the human being longs for justice as surely as he longs for meaning. Camus wrote in the fourth letter:

you saw the injustice of our condition to the point of being willing to add to it, whereas it seemed to me that man must exalt justice in order to fight against eternal injustice, create happiness in order to protest against the universe of unhappiness.[37]

The Germans not only accepted despair in the face of the absurd, but they made that despair their principle. Camus, however, refused "to accept that despair"; he "merely wanted men to rediscover their solidarity in order to wage war against their revolting fate."[38]

The two editorials from the underground *Combat* that have been definitively established as Camus's—but which, for reasons explained in the preface, are not included in this collection—are written along similar lines, although more simply and more directly. The Resistance fighters joined the struggle because of the "revolt and disgust" inspired in them by so many German atrocities. "For Total War, Total Resistance" (March 1944) reported several of those atrocities—including one in which an entire French village was burned simply because the Germans suspected that Resistance members had been allowed to hide there. Although the Germans were trying to divide France, they would succeed only in uniting the French people in common hatred against them, and more, in creating in the French people a force capable of changing the whole of France:

There are not two Frances, one fighting, the other judging the battle. . . . Tell yourself that we will all bear the great force of oppressed people, which is solidarity in suffering. This force will in turn put an end to lies; thereafter, our common hope is that it will still be strong enough to bring to life a new truth and a new France.

The editorial "For Three Hours They Gunned Down the French" (May 1944) reported the tragedy of Ascq, a small village in the north of France. After a German troop train had been derailed by an act of sabotage, the Germans marched into Ascq and summarily executed eighty-six of the villagers. "Out of the eighty men killed, most had never done anything to the Germans, and thought that nothing would be done to them. But France is united as one; there is only one anger, only one martyrdom." As for those Frenchmen inclined to collaborate with the Germans,

the question is not whether these crimes will be pardoned, but how they will be punished. . . . From now on, punishment for these crimes is the responsibility of the French people who, because of this massacre, will discover the solidarity of martrydom and the power of vengeance.

By August 1944 the advancing Allied armies had reached the outskirts of Paris. On the night of 20 August the Parisians rebelled against the occupiers, taking to the streets and putting up barricades. A "truce" had been negotiated on 17 August between General von Choltitz, the German military commander of Paris, and Pierre Taittinger, president of the Municipal Council, in order to let the Germans withdraw from the city peacefully. But contrary to Camus's editorial of 23 August, it was not the "assassins of the French" who broke the truce, but the Parisians themselves who, in their enthusiasm, refused to let the Germans escape from the city scot-free.[39]

Camus, along with the rest of the Resistance and most of

France, was emotionally overwhelmed by the victory. He felt that the Resistance, a small group of committed men and women, had gambled against overwhelming odds and won. Not only that, but their spirit of revolt had succeeded in infecting the working class of Paris, for it was the working class that fought the insurrection. They battled the Germans, Alexander Werth writes, "with old rifles, with pistols, with kitchen-knives, even; in the working-class areas barricades were springing up in every street." There were very few barricades, however, in the Champs-Elysées or other wealthy neighborhoods.[40]

Right and wrong must have suddenly seemed very obvious and clear in those days. Perhaps it even seemed that Sisyphus, for once, had succeeded in pushing his rock to the top of the mountain.

VI.

On 21 August, with Paris in a state of insurrection, *Combat* appeared above ground for the first time. Camus's front-page editorial bore as its title the motto of the underground *Combat:* "From Resistance to Revolution." The Resistance had fostered a new political force, Camus wrote, and those who had joined the Resistance "simply out of a modest sense of honor" had developed during the course of the struggle a political creed: "they started with faith alone, but now also have politics—in the best possible sense of that word. Having started with resistance, they now want to finish by revolution."

The Resistance leadership from the beginning had seen its struggle as a revolutionary and ideological struggle.[41] The Mouvements Unis de la Résistance had published a manifesto in the underground *Combat* in 1942 calling for a revolution in France after the war: "Our task will not end with the liberation of territory. Beyond that we want to rebuild France. We want to support the necessary contribution of France to Europe and the rest of the world."[42] In his editorial of 21 August 1944, and in other editorials during the following months, Camus's demands were along very similar lines as those formulated by the Resistance leadership during the Occupation: a Socialist form of government, broad economic and social reforms, and punishment of those responsible for the collapse of 1940 as well as those who had taken advantage of it.[43] "In the present state of things," he wrote, "this would be a revolution."

Camus believed that a society able to maintain the Resistance spirit after the Liberation might bring about a truly new order— one in which "politics is no longer dissociated from individuals" (*Combat*, 1 September 1944). Here at last was the chance to bring about significant and relatively lasting change. Camus maintained that continuing the "revolution" was every bit as important as continuing the war against the Germans, that the fight against the Germans was only the beginning of something greater: "The routines that were the fabric of political life before 1940 have ended. . . . the complicitous solidarity of politicians has been suppressed by the camaraderie of a struggle in which egoism has been abandoned" (1 September 1944). The new order would be made by and for the working class: "the role of the bourgeoisie as a ruling class ended in 1940" (6 September 1944).

The worst thing possible, Camus thought, would be to return to the old order that existed before the war, which "was never democracy but only its caricature" (2 September 1944). When the Socialists suggested shortly after the Liberation that at least some prewar leaders be included in the provisional government, Camus angrily rejected the proposal. The prewar leaders, he wrote, represented only betrayal and mediocrity; they "no longer have a place among us" (2 September 1944). Indeed, Camus advocated the purging of those who had capitulated to Vichy as well as those who had collaborated with Vichy and the Nazis.

Among the charges Camus leveled against the politicians of

the old order were "lack of imagination" and "political realism." These may at first not seem to be particularly serious crimes. But what Camus meant by "lack of imagination" was the complete failure on the part of politicians to see the suffering and indignities their policies brought to the everyday lives of common men. "Political realism" was the way in which the politicians rationalized their blindness and indifference: they claimed that politics was a complex process in which certain interests had to be suppressed in order to achieve long-range goals. The Vichy government claimed, for example, that they were playing a "double game," that they were only "pretending" to be allied with the Nazis because this would serve the long-term interests of France and even the Allies.

In his editorial of 19 September, Camus described the process by which revolt turns to revolution, thus foreshadowing the more complex distinction he would make between the two in *The Rebel:*

> Revolution is not revolt. What carried the Resistance for four years was revolt—the complete, obstinate, and at first nearly blind refusal to accept an order that would bring men to their knees. Revolt begins first in the human heart.
>
> But there comes a time when revolt spreads from heart to spirit, when a feeling becomes an idea, when impulse leads to concerted action. This is the moment of revolution.

In *The Rebel* Camus would write that revolt is an attitude that must be perpetually maintained, and that revolution is not a legitimate consequence of that attitude. Even in 1944 he did not believe in "definitive revolutions"; he stressed that the coming revolution should not be like those of 1789 and 1917, that it should be comparatively limited and comparatively peaceful. But he had not yet decided then that human action should be limited only to revolt. The Nazis and the Vichy politicians had forced the French to choose "either to kill or to kneel" (23 August 1944).

The Resistance fighters refused to kneel, and in their refusal they were asserting justice. This is why Camus felt justified in supporting the purge—even if, in extreme cases, the purge would require executions. In his editorial of 22 August, entitled "The Time of Justice," he wrote:

The men who deprived us of everything except shame, who forgave with one hand while they killed with the other, who added hypocrisy to terror, who during four years lived by a terrifying combination of moral sermons and executions, of homilies and torture, can expect from France neither oblivion nor indulgence. . . . We are not men of hate. But we require that those who killed and who permitted murder be held equally responsible in the name of the victims, even if those who tried to justify the murders speak today of the "double game" and of realism. This is the kind of language we despise most.

He added that "the voices of the tortured and the shamed have joined together to demand the most resolute justice" (2 November 1944).

Camus wrote that the purge must adhere to the principle of proportion: "What is a good purge? It is one that seeks to respect the general principle of justice without sacrificing the ability to judge individuals" (18 October 1944). It made no sense to punish civil servants severely while ignoring the leaders responsible for French industry and politics. Someone like Sacha Guitry, the actor who had been the darling of the Vichy leaders, would be sufficiently punished if he were never allowed to appear on stage again. On the other hand, those who were responsible for the worst crimes, those whose actions led to the deaths of their countrymen, must be punished by death.

Writing in the newspaper *Le Figaro*, François Mauriac, one of the two writers in the French Academy who had not backed Pétain in 1940, criticized Camus's support for the purge. Thus began an exchange of editorials by Camus and Mauriac on the subject of the purge and the death penalty. Mauriac wrote that he recognized the guilt of the collaborationists but made an appeal for clemency in the name of Christian charity. He asked whether human justice could really be impartial under the existing circumstances.[44] Camus responded by saying that the Christian could afford to indulge in forgiveness, for in the end he could appeal to divine justice. But for the nonbeliever, the choice was between silence and the pursuit of human justice. Therefore Camus chose "human justice with all its terrible imperfections; we can hope to make it better only by holding desperately to our honesty" (25 October 1944). Camus added that he would "refuse forever a divine charity which frustrates the justice of men" (11 January 1945).

Camus continued to believe throughout the autumn of 1944 that the Resistance movement would evolve into an important political movement with a concrete and revolutionary program. But things were not going well. Shortly after the Liberation the leftist groups that had been able to unite in concerted effort against Vichy and the Nazis began to disagree on basic political issues. Moreover, there was "latent conflict" between the provisional government and the Resistance organizations; de Gaulle himself "was clearly out of sympathy with the Home Resistance."[45] French politics lapsed more and more into the pre-Vichy forms.

Combat, along with the rest of the Resistance, was accused by critics of being unable to formulate any definite political line. It is true that Camus's proposals for bringing about the political renovation he demanded were quite vague. His frequent assertion that France must reconcile freedom with justice—to give each individual as much freedom as possible while still maintaining justice for all—was hardly a concrete or original idea. In his editorial of 1 October 1944, Camus responded to the accusations of vagueness: "Our plan is to make justice reign through the economy and to guarantee freedom through politics. . . .

what we want for France is a collectivist economy and a liberal political structure." But this was only slightly less vague than what he had written before.

In November Camus gave his qualified support to the Socialist Party. After all, Camus wrote, the hopes and ideals of nearly all France seemed to be embodied by the Socialist Party program. The reason so many Frenchmen hesitated to back the Socialist Party was because of its past, which had often showed it to be "more lavish with words than keen on action." Indeed, the Socialists still had a tendency to confuse "the goal of realizing their ideals with that of obtaining a majority in the Assembly." Nonetheless, if the Socialist Party could succeed in truly reforming itself, as it seemed to be trying to do, then Camus was convinced that the party could be "the great force of tomorrow's French society" (10 November 1944).

But by December, Camus was already expressing serious doubts that any major change would come from the "revolution." He quoted an 1868 speech by Edgar Quinet beginning, "Once a revolution has broken out, what must you do to ruin it?" Camus felt that once again politicians had manipulated the people with rhetoric, that they had tricked the people into abandoning their revolutionary impulses.

More important, it was becoming increasingly clear to Camus that the purge was, as all purges tend to be, an arbitrary bloodletting. Werth sardonically calls the purge trials "the circuses to which an underfed population was treated during that hard winter of 1944–45."[46] Many notorious collaborationists, particularly lesser known bankers and industrialists, were given light sentences or were not even indicted, whereas minor journalists could often expect stiff prison sentences or even the death penalty. In the provinces, alleged collaborationists were often shot without benefit of trial. Many executions seemed to be little more than political or personal vendettas.[47] Werth estimates that the number of summary executions carried out after the Liberation was well into the thousands.[48] Camus, in his editorial of 5 January 1945, wrote that the purge was indeed going badly and "that now it is probably too late for justice to be done."

In mid-January Camus, exhausted from work and ill, took a one-month leave from *Combat*. During that month he made an important decision. He was asked to sign a petition requesting the commutation of the death sentence for Robert Brasillach, a well-known novelist and critic who during the war had made anti-Semitic and pro-Nazi denunciations in the collaborationist newspaper *Je suis partout*. Camus paced the floor all night before finally deciding to sign.[49] This was clearly a change from the position he had taken in his *Combat* editorials not long before. It must have been then that Camus decided he would oppose the death penalty in all circumstances, even for men whose crimes had caused the deaths of Camus's own comrades. (The petition, also signed by Mauriac, Jean Anouilh, Jean Cocteau, Colette, and others, was rejected; Brasillach was executed by firing squad.)

Camus returned to *Combat* in February to write one editorial in which he confirmed that *Combat* had not given up the principles that had inspired the Resistance fighters during the Occupation and Liberation; but he noted that, whereas six months ago *Combat* was part of a widespread consensus, it now seemed to be part of a minority opposition. Camus concluded that "what has changed is not our convictions, but rather the intentions of our government" (9 February 1945). Camus wrote no more editorials until mid-May; whether he had taken another leave from *Combat* is uncertain. He did write for *Combat* throughout the summer of 1945, and among his editorials was his condemnation of the purge (30 August 1945), in which he wrote that the purge had become both a failure and a disgrace, and asked that the flagrant injustices committed in its name be discontinued.

After that summer, Camus took a year-long leave to work on *The Plague*. He returned in November 1946 and contributed the series of articles entitled "Neither Victims nor Executioners." He again took up his duties as full-time editor in March 1947, after a debilitating month-long printers' strike. In June *Combat* was sold to Henri Smadja, and Camus resigned.

VII.

In *The Plague* a small group of men recognize the dangers of the plague as soon as it strikes their city, and despite the overwhelming indifference of nearly everyone else, begin what will be a long, exhausting, and deadly struggle. They continue to fight the plague, not knowing whether their efforts are having any real effect; but they know that not to fight it would be to accept it, to be accomplices in the suffering it causes. As the plague grows worse, more and more men join this group. The journalist Rambert who, like Camus, was cut off from his wife and family and did not recognize the evils of the plague from the start, joins the fight. But even at the end of the plague, this group represents only a small part of the city's population, though nearly everyone rejoices when the plague is over.

Revolt in *The Stranger* was the struggle of the individual to give his own life meaning in the face of death. Revolt in *The Plague* is a common struggle by individuals against a common fate they know they share with other human beings. Their efforts may be no less futile than Meursault's, yet at the same time, the small possibility exists that they may improve the lives of those around them. Revolt becomes a reason for solidarity and participation.

While the analogy between the plague and the Nazi Occupation is clear enough, the analogy is not unproblematic. As Sartre and others pointed out, the French Resistance fighters, unlike those who fought the plague, had to make a choice whether or not to kill other men. But when Roland Barthes called *The Plague* a "refusal of history" and asked what Camus would do if faced with the destruction of human beings rather than the destruction of microbes, Camus replied that he and the other Resistance fighters had already answered that question.[50] The evil of the Nazis—the suffering they caused—was so great and obvious that the only alternative was to fight it. The Resistance fighters were *forced* to kill, and thus their consciences could be as clear as the consciences of those who fought the plague. And Camus knew that tyranny, like the plague microbe, could return at any time, and that if it did, men would again be forced either to kill or to accept the nihilism and suffering that tyranny inevitably brings.

Camus's novel also said that the plague and evils like it cause men to rise above themselves. But once the evil is defeated, there is a problem that the novel did not consider: the hero, having risen above himself, may be left with a certain headiness, that is, a sense of moral superiority. Once the victimizer has been over-thrown, the overwhelming temptation—to which Camus himself had succumbed—is for the victim to become his former oppressor's judge and executioner.

Camus looked back on the months after the Liberation as representing perhaps the darkest moment of his life. He had written in *Combat* that France must be made "pure," and so for the sake of an ideal—and an illusory one at that—he had argued in favor of the death penalty. In a speech made to the Dominican monastery of Latour-Mauberg in 1948, he spoke of his exchange of editorials with François Mauriac:

Three years ago, a controversy put me up against one among you—certainly not the least formidable. The fever of those years, the painful memories of my murdered friends, are what led me to the position I took. I can say here that, despite some excessively harsh language on the part of François Mauriac, I have never stopped thinking about what he said. At the end of my reflection—and I tell you this to show how useful I find the dialogue between believer and nonbeliever—I have come to admit to myself and to admit publicly here that on the central issue of our argument, M. Mauriac was right and I was wrong.[51]

And Camus wrote in "Neither Victims nor Executioners": "I will never again be among those who, for whatever reasons, accommodate themselves to murder, and . . . I accept the consequences of my choice" (30 November 1946).

In "Neither Victims nor Executioners" Camus wrote that a third way must be found between that of the victim and that of the victimizer. He also wrote, as he had done earlier in *Combat*, that Europe must find a third way between American capitalism and Soviet communism (though clearly he finds the latter more oppressive and dangerous). The terms Camus uses and the conclusions to which he comes in this series of articles are very similar to those of *The Rebel*.

Camus wrote in "Neither Victims nor Executioners" that those who live in a world of absolute ends think that murder is legitimized. What is worse, perhaps, is that, because the absolutists consider everything as means for achieving ends *which have been predetermined,* there is no reason for even discussing the means. "The long dialogue among men," wrote Camus, "has just come to an end. Naturally, a man who will not listen is a man to be feared" (19 November 1946).

But Camus insisted that all those who are still capable must resume the dialogue. The question of legitimized murder must be addressed, for if one accepts legitimized murder, then one consents to being either a victim or a perpetrator of violence. Camus did not ask for a world in which murder does not exist, for he knew such a world is impossible; but he did ask for a world in which murder is not legitimized.

To those who accused him of being utopian, Camus admitted

29

that the forces of dialogue seem to have little chance of prevailing over the forces of violence. But his is a "relative utopia." Indeed, the Marxist and capitalist ideologies are "both convinced that the application of their principles will inevitably lead to a harmonious society" and are therefore "utopian to a far greater degree." Moreover, the Marxist and capitalist visions of utopia cost lives, whereas Camus's relative utopia does not (20 November 1946).

Camus still expressed hope for socialism, but wrote that the Socialists must first abandon Marxism as an absolute philosophy. Because the world has been divided between the American and Soviet empires, any attempted revolution from either side would mean war. The advanced technology of weapons promises that such a war would mean near-total annihilation. Marxist thought is thus outdated, for Marx did not foresee that the destructiveness of modern weapons would make violent revolution impossible. If one still insists on balancing the means against the ends, then one must measure the cost of a world war against whatever progress a world war might promise. Camus concludes:

No matter what the desired goal, no matter how lofty or necessary it seems, no matter if it promises happiness, justice, and freedom, the means used to reach it represent such an enormous risk and are so greatly disproportionate to the chances of success that we must refuse them. (26 November 1946)

As Camus later wrote in *The Rebel,* revolution's "chances are balanced against the risks of a universal war, which, even in the event of victory, will only present it with an Empire of ruins." [52]

The world is moving fast, Camus concluded in "Neither Victims nor Executioners," and our old ways of thinking are becoming increasingly outdated. Soon even the clash of American and Soviet empires will be superseded by the clash of civilization: "Everywhere the colonial peoples are demanding that their voices be heard. Perhaps in ten years, perhaps in fifty, the pre-eminence of Western civilization will be in question" (27 November 1946). We might as well prepare for that now, Camus reasoned, by establishing a true international democracy in the form of a world parliament in which all peoples are represented equally.

However, Camus wrote, one could not count on the current governments for such moderate and well-reasoned solutions, for the current governments "live and act according to murderous principles." Rather, "men . . . as individuals" must "create among themselves, both within and across borders, a new social contract which will unite men according to more reasonable principles" (29 November 1946).

The articles end with Camus again asking for dialogue, for men who think like himself to come forward and speak out in order to oppose fear and silence. Their chances for success were slim, Camus admitted, but "I have always thought that if the man who places hope in the human condition is a fool, then he who gives up hope in the face of circumstances is a coward" (30 November 1946).

Camus continued his pleas for moderation and dialogue in *The Rebel* in 1951, though here he formulated his argument in terms of rebellion. Even in *The Myth of Sisyphus*, rebellion had been ultimately a protest against death. Camus reasoned in *The Rebel* that true rebellion can never lead to death but must always seek to preserve life. Murder as well as suicide are illegitimate. "[M]urder and rebellion are contradictory," he wrote. "Rebellion is in itself moderation." [53]

VIII.

It is clear, then, that the war years and the months immediately following the Liberation had a profound effect on Camus's thinking. The experiences of the Occupation led him to believe that revolt was an assertion of justice. The experiences of the Liberation convinced him that this assertion of justice must have its limits. Such are the conclusions of *The Rebel*.

Politics always tended to be a stormy affair for Camus, and the publication of *The Rebel* was no exception. After *The Rebel* appeared, the book and Camus himself were attacked by Sartre and other writers of the Left, many of whom had been Camus's comrades in the Resistance. Emmanuel d'Astier de la Vigerie had told Camus, in response to "Neither Victims nor Executioners": "You shun politics and take refuge in morality."[54] The accusations against *The Rebel* were basically the same: that Camus's experiment with politics during the Liberation had obviously left him with a bad taste in his mouth, so that now he chose to be above politics. Francis Jeanson, in a sharply critical review in Sartre's journal *Les Temps modernes*, wrote that the book was "transcendental" and "antihistorical," that in it Camus chose metaphysics over politics. When Camus wrote an equally sharp reply to *Les Temps modernes*, asserting that his book could be considered antihistorical only if rewritten that way by the reviewer,[55] he addressed the reply not to Jeanson but to "monsieur le directeur," Sartre himself. Sartre's "Reply to Albert Camus," which appeared in the same issue as Camus's "Letter to the Director," has earned notoriety "for some of the most acrid *ad hominem* argumentation in twentieth-century writing."[56] Among other things, Sartre wrote:

Your combination of dreary conceit and vulnerability always discouraged people from telling you unvarnished truths. The result is that you have become the victim of a dismal self-importance. . . . Tell me, Camus, for what mysterious reasons may your works not be discussed without taking away humanity's reasons for living? By what miracle are the objections made to you transformed within the hour, into sacrilege? . . . You are no longer anything but an abstraction of revolt. . . . Your morality first changed into moralism. Today it is only literature. Tomorrow perhaps it will be immorality.[57]

Sartre's reply abruptly ended the Camus-Sartre friendship that had existed, often uneasily, since the early 1940s. It also effectively ostracized Camus from the Parisian intellectual community.

In 1954 the Algerian Moslems revolted against the French colonialists. The Algerian revolution soon became "on both sides one of the bloodiest and most ruthless colonial wars of modern times."[58] Camus's refusal to support the Moslems further convinced his critics that he was "too fastidious to dirty his hands in the real stuff of politics."[59] Yet in the 1930s Camus had been one of the first Frenchmen to protest the Moslems' misery. Shortly after World War II, he had predicted violent uprisings unless strenuous measures were taken to correct that misery.[60] And in 1956 Camus would travel to Algeria to try to work out a peaceful solution.

Camus's position toward the Algerian War was entirely in keeping with the conclusions he had reached in "Neither Victims nor Executioners" and *The Rebel*. He sympathized with the Moslems' cause but would not support violence as a means to pursue it. "There are other ways of establishing necessary justice," he wrote, "than to replace one form of injustice by another."[61] Sartre and other French leftists saw the Algerian conflict purely as an anticolonial struggle. Given the Moslems' suffering and oppression under the French colonial system, their use of extreme violence was both comprehensible and justified.[62] To Camus's mind, the leftist position exemplified all the blindness and irresponsible romanticism of ideologues. There were one million Frenchmen in Algeria, many of whom were Algerian-born and of the working class. "Must these hardworking Frenchmen," Camus asked, "be offered up for the slaughter to atone for the enormous sins of colonialist France?"[63]

Camus's 1956 trip to Algeria to appeal for a truce was a complete failure. He was generally derided by both sides; the French Algerians whom he sought to protect were especially hostile, greeting him with cries of "Camus to the gallows!" After this, Camus seldom commented on the Algerian situation, though in 1958 he did publish a selection of his journalistic writings on Algeria, *Actuelles III*. He told his friend Jean Bloch-Michel in 1959 that when a referendum on Algerian independence took place, he would ask for space in an Algiers newspaper and campaign for self-determination but against complete independence.[64] But shortly thereafter he confided to Bloch-Michel that he had given up hope that the Moslems would accept anything less than total independence from France.[65] As to how Camus would have reacted when Algerian independence did come in 1962, one can only speculate, for he died in January 1960 in a car accident in the south of France.

The accusations that Camus believed himself above politics must have stung him, for despite his distaste for it, he was intensely involved with politics all his life. He wrote in his notebook in 1948: "modern man is obliged to be concerned with politics. I am concerned with it, in spite of myself and because, through my defects rather than through my virtues, I have never been able to refuse any of the obligations I encountered."[66]

Camus, however, did come to feel that, when writing for *Combat* during the first months of the Liberation, he had been carried away by his passionate aspirations for what society might achieve. He subsequently concluded that society as a whole could do little to improve itself. Instead, he decided to appeal to the individual, for it was the individual, he believed, who represented society's greatest hope. The Resistance, after all, had been made up of a small group of individuals, a minority in their society. It is true that they could not rightly claim to have saved France on their own. But they could rightly claim to have saved France's moral integrity and honor.

Camus's work, including *The Rebel*, is at its core more concerned with personal ethics than political philosophy. As he said when he received the Nobel Prize for Literature in 1956: "By definition, [the writer] cannot serve those who make history: he serves those who have to live it." [67]

Part I

COMBAT, FROM RESISTANCE TO REVOLUTION

Combat Continues . . .

21 August 1944

Today, 21 August, as we appear in the open for the first time, the liberation of Paris has been achieved. After fifty months of occupation, of struggle and sacrifice, Paris is reborn to the sense of freedom, despite the shots suddenly exploding in the streets.

But it would be dangerous to resume life with the illusion that freedom of the individual comes without effort and pain. Freedom must be deserved and must be won. It is by combat against invaders and traitors that the French Forces of the Interior [1] are here restoring the Republic, which is inseparable from freedom. It is by combat that freedom and the Republic will triumph.

The liberation of Paris is only one step toward the liberation of France, and here the word LIBERATION must be taken in its broadest sense. Combat against Nazi Germany continues; it will continue relentlessly. But even if this is the hardest of struggles for which all France has mobilized, it is not the only one we must fight.

It will not be enough to return to the mere appearance of liberty with which the France of 1939 had to be content. We will have accomplished only an infinitesimal part of our task if tomorrow's French Republic finds itself, like the Third Republic, confined by the domination of Money.

We all know that the fight against the privileges of money was always a favorite theme of Pétain and his crew.[2] But we also know that, since July 1940, Money has weighed more heavily on our people than ever before. For that is when Money, to conserve and increase its privileges, hoisted traitors to power and deliberately tied its interests to Hitler's.

It is not by accident that we have seen as advisers to the Vichy ministers a succession of Lavals, Bouthiliers, Badouins, Pucheus, Leroy-Laduries. It is not by accident that the so-called principal committees of "organization" have been led by "organizers" whose relationship to the proletariat have been, in most cases, nothing but the relationship of masters to servants.

Through the struggle we wage with the Allies against Hitler's armies, all French territory will soon be liberated. The Allies have made our liberation possible. But our freedom is our own; it is we who must shape it.

Combat continues . . .

They Will Not Escape

23 August 1944

What is an insurrection? It is the people in arms. Who are the people? They are those in a nation who will never be made to kneel.

A nation is worth what its people are worth. If we have been tempted to doubt our country, the image of our sons standing straight, their fists raised with rifles, fills us with the overwhelming certainty that this nation is equal to its greatest destinies, that France will achieve its renaissance at the same time it regains its liberty.

On the fourth day of insurrection, after the first retreat of the enemy, after a day of false truce broken by the assassins of the French,[3] the Parisian people will put up barricades and continue the fight.

The enemy entrenched in the city must not be allowed to leave. The enemy in retreat who try to enter the city must not be allowed to penetrate. They will not escape.

A very few among us, crippled in their imagination and memories, forgetful of honor, and unconcerned with shame, sit in their personal comfort and ask, "What will this accomplish?" We must answer them here.

A people who want to live free do not wait for someone to bring their freedom. They take it. In so doing, they help themselves as well as those who would come to their aid. Each German who does not leave Paris means a bullet saved for the Allied soldiers and for our French comrades in the East. Our future, our revolution are here now in their entirety, filled with the cries of anger, passion, and freedom.

It is not we who wanted to kill. But we have been forced either to kill or to kneel. Though they tried to make us forget, we know now, after four years of terrible struggle, that we are not a race that kneels. Although they still want to make us forget, we know also that we are a great nation. And a great nation takes its destiny in hand, in proud times as well as in times of shame.

We know what it is like to carry the weight of defeat; it is not before the burden of victory that we will fall. On 21 August 1944, in the streets of Paris, a battle has begun for all of us and all France that will end in liberty or death.

The Age of Scorn

30 August 1944

Thirty-four Frenchmen tortured and then murdered at Vincennes. These would be meaningless words were it not for the picture they provoke in our imagination. What does the picture look like? Two men face to face, one of whom prepares to tear off the fingernails of the other who watches him do it.

This is hardly the first time that such unbearable images confront us. In 1933 began the era that one of the greatest among us called "the age of scorn."[4] For the ten years since, our minds have reeled at every story of naked and defenseless human beings systematically mutilated by men who, in appearance, were no different from ourselves. We have asked how it could be possible.

Yet it was possible. For ten years it was possible, and as if to serve notice that our military victory is not complete, today there are more comrades butchered, their bodies mangled, their eyes crushed under boot heels. Those guilty of such crimes doffed their hats and gave their seats to old ladies in the metro; just like Himmler, they made torture a science and a business, then came home at night through the back door so as not to awaken their favorite pet canary.

Yes, we know all too well that it was possible. But so much is possible; why have we chosen to speak of this and not other things? Because this is a matter of killing the spirit and humiliating the soul. Those dedicated to the use of force understand their enemy. They know that a thousand rifles aimed at a man will not stop him from believing in the justice of his cause, and that when he is dead, there will be other just men to say "no" until force itself is worn out. Killing the just man, then, is not enough. They must break his spirit, too, so that the example of a just man giving up on human dignity will discourage all just men and even justice itself.

For ten years a nation dedicated itself to this destruction of souls. They were convinced enough of their strength to believe that the soul would be their only obstacle, so they busied themselves with the soul. To their misfortune, they were often successful in their work. They knew that there is always an hour of the day and night when even the bravest men feel like cowards.

They always knew to wait for that hour, and when that hour came, they hunted the soul through the wounds of the body. They left the soul haggard and crazed, and sometimes they made of it a traitor and a liar.

Who would dare speak here of forgiveness? Since the spirit finally understood that a sword is needed to conquer a sword, and since the spirit took up the sword and attained victory, who would ask it to forget? It is not hatred that will speak tomorrow, but justice itself, based firmly on memory. And it is the most eternal and sacred justice which will perhaps forgive those among us who, with the peace of a heart that never betrayed, died without having spoken. But justice will strike hard against the most courageous of us who in their acts of cowardice degraded their souls and died desperate, carrying in their forever ravaged hearts hatred for others and scorn for themselves.

Critique of the New Press

31 August 1944

Because today represents a moment of respite between the insurrection and the war, I have chosen to write on a subject that I know well and that is close to my heart: the press. And because I am thinking specifically of the press that has emerged out of the battle of Paris, I must also discuss the fraternity and clarity that we owe our comrades in combat.

When we were printing our newspapers underground, we worked, of course, without much ceremony and without declarations of policy. But I know that all our comrades on all our papers worked with a great and secret hope: that all those who continually risked death for the sake of a few ideals they held dear would be able to give their country the press it deserved but no longer had. We knew firsthand that the press before the war had lost both its sense of principles and its morality. The appetite for money and the indifference to things of greatness had conspired to give France a press that, with a few rare exceptions, sought only to increase the power of a minority and in so doing diminished the morality of all. It is therefore not difficult to see how this press came to be what it was during the years 1940−44, which is to say, the shame of our country.

Our desire, all the more profound because there was so seldom a means to express it, was to free the press from money and to give it a voice and a truth that would help our readers achieve a level where the best in them would be brought out. We thought that a country is worth whatever its press is worth. And if it is true that the press represents the voice of a nation, we hoped to do whatever small part we could to raise this nation by elevating the level of its language. Right or wrong, these were the reasons for which many of us died in unimaginable conditions or suffered the solitude and peril of prisons.

Now we have occupied buildings from which we have published our newspapers in the midst of battle. We have won a great victory. The journalists of the Resistance have shown courage and determination and for this deserve everyone's respect. But—and forgive me for writing this when there is such enormous enthusiasm—all this means little because there is so much left to accomplish. We have won the means by which to achieve the great revolution that all of us desire; now we must actually achieve it. And to sum it up, Paris's liberated press, such as we have seen after a dozen or so issues, leaves much to be desired.

I hope that what I am trying to say in this article, and in the articles that follow, will be taken in the spirit in which it is intended. I speak in the name of the fraternity of our common struggle; these comments are directed at no one in particular. Criticism is applicable to the entire press without exception—including *Combat*.

But is it too early for such criticism? Should we give our papers time to get organized before subjecting them to such scrupulous examination? The answer is no. We are in a good position to know the incredible conditions under which our papers are produced. But this is not a question of production. Rather, it is a question of a certain voice that should have been taken from the beginning, yet never was. The time for the press to submit itself to self-examination is the very time when the press is defining itself, when it is searching for its definitive form. The press must decide what it wants to be and then become it.

And what do we want? A press with clarity and strength, with language that demands respect. This is a question of men who during these past years wrote articles knowing that their only remuneration could well be prison or death. Such men know the value of words; they know that words must be chosen carefully.

This is the responsibility of the journalist to the society he wants to rebuild.

The Sin of Laziness

Now, in the haste, anger, and delirium of our offensive, our newspapers sin by their laziness. The body of our press has worked so hard that its spirit has lost its vigilance. Many of our papers are once again appearing in forms that we believed obsolete. They avoid neither excessive rhetoric nor the shop-girl mentality that was the distinctive mark of our papers both before and after the outbreak of war.

First, we do not want to be only a poor imitation of the prewar press. Second, we do not want lethargy to return us to the same formulas and ideas that threatened to destroy the morality of the press and of the country. We shall not abandon or give up hope for what we have to achieve.

Now that we have obtained the methods for self-expression, we owe complete responsibility to ourselves and to our country. What is essential—and this is the point of this article—is that we maintain our vigilance. All of us have the following task: to reflect carefully on what we intend to say; to mold our papers bit by bit; to write attentively and never lose sight of the enormous necessity of giving our country a powerful and ample voice. If we can make that voice one of energy rather than hate, of proud objectivity rather than rhetoric, of humanity rather than mediocrity, then much can be saved and we shall not have proved ourselves unworthy.

Resistance and Politics

1 September 1944

Before this war, one spoke of the world of politics. This world may have had its connections to the world of arts or finance, but it also had its own people, its own traditions and prejudices, and occasionally its own greatness.

One did not enter this world without an apprenticeship. The training provided by working for a political party or office was a good education. One learned that success or failure came according to a game of imponderables, which might make those with imaginative spirits suspect the existence of some vast but secret network of influence. Stars were suddenly born, premieres anxiously awaited. Ambassadors and ladies of Society sat high on the rostrums of political assemblies.

The problem that exists today in France is not only for institutions and authorities. The problem involves everyone. All those of us who participated in the Resistance knew that, because danger is contagious and because the Germans practiced blackmail, our families, friends, and even strangers with no other connection than our common cause, were often put unknowingly at risk. We accepted these risks in their totality and with full awareness. Thus the conviction was formed that political struggle is not a career, or a game, or an accident of birth.

Of course the Resistance did not begin as a political struggle. The fight against the Vichy government was only a consequence of the fight against the occupier. But under the conditions of clandestine action, war took on a new form. Our military machine had to be constructed out of many different pieces. Such an undertaking is of a political nature. Committing sabotage is an act of war. But bringing together the saboteurs, co-ordinating throughout the country activities carried out by people and groups with different social backgrounds—this is an act of politics.

The privilege of the Resistance is not to call upon forces that are already unified, and whose services are channeled by politics into achieving its goals. Rather, its privilege is to awaken society's dormant forces, which are the forces of the individual. The routines that were the fabric of political life before 1940 have ended; the men who joined the Resistance found themselves in the solitary position of choosing shame or action.

So a tradition that is essentially humane takes the place of a tradition that was exclusively political, in the social as well as in the political order. Not that the political action of the Resistance was ever anarchic. But the complicitous solidarity of politicians has been suppressed by the camaraderie of a struggle in which egoism has been abandoned.

A new order has been founded. It is an order in which the face of man is seen in bright light. Politics is no longer dissociated from individuals. It is addressed directly by man to other men. It is a way of speaking. If the Resistance is remembered as more than just a moment in our history, it will be remembered for having placed our citizens face to face.

To Make Democracy

2 September 1944

As we have said before, there is a problem of government. It is, to a great extent, our problem, as it is indeed the problem of everyone. But if we have yet to say exactly what our position is, it is because we thought it best to have confidence in those who until now have been representing France abroad. We thought that these men would see immediately what needs to be done, especially with the advice of those who defended France at home. We think so still.

But others are making their positions known, and what they say surprises us. Because we do not believe in politics without clear language, we shall say here what we think.

Our comrades at *Le Populaire* reported a meeting between General de Gaulle and the general secretary of the Socialist Party. The latter advocates the formation of a government that would be "a mixture of veteran statesmen—assuring the continuity of the Republic and doctrinal solidarity with yesterday's democracy—and new men whose presence in the government would assure the rejuvenation that is being demanded throughout the country."

We have in common with our Socialist comrades enough struggles and hopes to believe ourselves justified when we say that this wording, in itself, is inadequate. But what it allows, because it is imprecise, worries us even more.

We are perplexed by the inclusion of these "veteran statesmen," who, to be brief, have not performed so brilliantly that we would note our solidarity with them. Many of them have betrayed France, willfully or out of weakness. The rest of them, though they did not betray France, failed to serve it. They no longer have a place among us.

True, we realize that, abroad as well as at home, we need to show signs of moderation. France, for its own sake and for the sake of its friends, must put itself in order. But we must consider: what kind of order?

An order that would mark the return to the persons and regime that collapsed at the shock of war, to a parliament whose great majority capitulated to Pétain, to a system which consecrated the privileges of money and the wedding of political lobbies with personal ambitions—this order would be nothing but disorder, because it would consolidate injustice.

Order comes when the people consent. Unless the terrible experiences of these four years have been in vain, unless our hopes were baseless delusions and our faith a mockery, the people will not consent to the return of those who deserted us when we needed them most. We can be sure that those who fought with the Resistance will never consent.

The way to assure disorder is to attempt to bring back, under the vain pretext of restoring democracy, that tainted and mediocre order represented by M. Chautemps, M. Chichery,[5] and the many others. We are angered that, after all that has happened, we have to repeat: the old order with which they would start all over again today was never democracy but only its caricature.

As for true democracy, we will have to make it ourselves. And this we will do with order, a true order, of people united and resolved to survive. In this order each will receive his due, which means these "veteran statesmen," who inspire only indifference or scorn, can always put themselves to work writing memoirs destined never to be read.

Justice and Freedom

8 September 1944

In yesterday's *Le Figaro*, M. d'Ormesson commented on the recent speech by the Pope. This speech has already provoked quite a few remarks. But M. d'Ormesson's commentary at least has the merit of posing clearly the problem that faces Europe today.

"It is a question," he says, "of bringing about a harmony between the freedom of the individual, which is more necessary, more sacred than ever, and the collective organization of society, which has made inevitable certain conditions of modern life."

This is well put. We propose to M. d'Ormesson only a simpler formula in saying that the question for all of us is how to reconcile justice with freedom. The goal we must pursue is to make life free for the individual, but just for all. Other countries have striven for this but have been only partially successful, having put freedom before justice or the other way around. The task for France must be to seek a truer balance.

We do not deny that such balance is difficult. If we look at history, we see that it has not yet been possible, that between freedom and justice there seems to exist a state of contradiction. How could there not be? Freedom for each also means freedom for the rich and ambitious; that invites injustice. Justice for all means the submission of the individual to the collective good. How can we speak, then, of absolute freedom?

M. d'Ormesson believes that Christianity provides the solution. We hope that he will permit a nonbeliever, who is nonetheless respectful of others' convictions, to express his doubts. Christianity is in its essence (and this is its paradoxical greatness) a doctrine of injustice. It is based on the sacrifice of an innocent and it accepts this sacrifice. But as Paris has just shown with its nights lit by flames of insurrection, justice does not come without revolt.

So must we give up our efforts to reconcile the irreconcilable? No, we must never abandon them, but simply understand the immense difficulties involved. And we must point these difficulties out to those who, in good faith, would oversimplify everything.

For the rest, let it be known that this is the one effort in today's world which makes life worth living and fighting for. Under conditions so desperate, the hard, marvelous task of this century is to create justice in the most unjust of worlds, and to protect freedom from those souls who, out of principle, choose servitude. If we fail, man will return to darkness. But at least we will have fought to find light.

This effort demands clearsightedness and that prompt vigilance which will keep us from thinking of the individual when we should be thinking of all, or from thinking of society as a whole when it is the individual who cries out for our help. M. d'Ormesson is correct in thinking that the Christian, thanks to his love of his fellow man, can maintain such a difficult effort. But so can those who lack faith but have selflessness, a simple concern for the truth, and a taste for human greatness.

The Journalistic Critique

8 September 1944

We must aspire to a journalism of ideas. As we have noted before, the idea of the French press doing little more than grinding out information leaves something to be desired. If we seek to inform quickly rather than to inform well, the truth will not be served.

One can reasonably regret, then, that most editorials accord information a place it should not occupy. At least one thing is obvious: information as provided to the newspapers, and as the newspapers use it, cannot do without critical commentary. This rule could improve the entire press.

The journalist could add to a better understanding of the news through commentary showing the import of information of which neither the source nor the intention is always clear. He could, for example, present two dispatches side by side, each contradicting the other. He could enlighten his readership on the amount of credibility to be accorded to certain information, knowing that information came from a specific press agency or foreign bureau. There is no doubt that among the myriad bureaus maintained abroad by the press agencies before the war, only four or five could be depended on to provide the truth required by a press fulfilling its proper role. Thus the journalist, better informed than the rest of the public, must use information that he knows to be questionable with the greatest reserve.

To this direct critique of both text and sources, the journalist could add clear and precise exposés educating the public on the technique of information. Just because the average reader wants to know about Doctor Petiot[6] and jewel swindling does not mean that he is uninterested in the operation of the international press. It would be better to try to awake the reader's critical instincts than to appeal to his laziness. The only question is whether this critique of information is technically possible. My conviction on this point is total.

There is another contribution the journalist must make to the public: political and moral commentary on daily events. In the face of history's disordered forces, it is important to note from time to time the thoughts of a man of conscience or the common observations of several men of conscience. But that cannot be done without scruples, and without a certain notion of relativity. To be sure, a taste for truth does not eliminate bias. Yet if what we try to do in this newspaper begins to be understood, bias will

not be heard without a balance of the truth. But here as elsewhere there is a voice to discover; without this voice, all will be
cheapened.

Let us take some examples in the press today. It is now clear
that, with the astonishing speed of the Allied troops and worldwide developments, the certitude of victory has replaced the in-
defatigable hope of liberation. At long last, peace approaches.
Thus our newspapers are forced to define immediately what the
country is and wants. That is why there is such a question of
France in their articles. Of course this is a subject that one can
approach only with infinite care and by choosing words carefully. It would add little to the definition we seek, if we returned
to clichés and patriotic phrases from the time when the French
got angry at the very mention of a word like "fatherland." Yet
these are the very words we are hearing once again. For new
times there must be, if not new words, at least new definitions for
old ones. In seeking to put things in order, we have only our
hearts to guide us and the respect that gives genuine love. Only at
this price will we do our small part by giving the country the language that will make it listen.

What we ask is that articles have substance and depth, and
that false or doubtful news not be presented as the truth. This series of steps is what I call the Journalistic Critique. It requires a
certain voice and a lot of sacrifice. For now, at least, it is something to start thinking about.

[The N.L.M.'s first public meeting]

19 September 1944

The National Liberation Movement[7] has held its first public meeting. There, men who did not speak on behalf of a political party and who came forth owing no allegiance to any group that existed before the war, were hailed by a considerable number of the French people. It has not, perhaps, been remarked that such support is something new. Nor has it been properly acknowledged that these men, who for four years spoke only of France, spoke yesterday of revolution.

Let us try to understand: what kind of revolution did they mean? The revolution as discussed Sunday at Pleyel bears little resemblance to revolutions proposed before the war and by very different groups. That is why, to some, the discussion seemed vague. They are used to hearing words that recall the familiar images. Revolution for many means 1789 and 1917. The rest is too tiresome to think about. We are not even sure that those who spoke yesterday have themselves a really precise image of the form this revolution is to take. But they speak in the name of an inner force which has carried them for four years, but which extends beyond the speakers and, under the right circumstances, could take on its true form tomorrow.

Revolution is not revolt. What carried the Resistance for four years was revolt—the complete, obstinate, and at first nearly blind refusal to accept an order that would bring men to their knees. Revolt begins first in the human heart.

But there comes a time when revolt spreads from heart to spirit, when a feeling becomes an idea, when impulse leads to concerted action. This is the moment of revolution.

The French Resistance, in its original form, started in the purity of total refusal. But four years of struggle have brought it the ideas it lacked. At the end of triumphant revolt comes the desire for revolution. And if the breath of revolt is not cut short, it will produce a revolution accompanied by the clear and original thinking we await. We believe it is possible to describe the basic principles of this revolution, and we will soon return to this task.

But for the moment we are satisfied, despite the skeptics and despite uncertainty over the exact form revolution will take, that there exists in France the general desire for revolution. We do not, however, believe in definitive revolutions. All human effort is relative. The unjust law of history is that man makes enormous sacrifices for results that are often absurdly small. Even so, man reaches toward his truths; his progress may be slow, but we think it justifies all sacrifices.

Come what may, the unformed ideas finally bursting forth after four years of night must not be underestimated. In them are the beginnings of light and rebirth.

Those who doubt us will perhaps be proven right tomorrow. But today they are wrong, for they give themselves up to laziness of spirit and imagine that history does not renew itself.

Revolution is not necessarily the guillotine and machine guns; rather, it is machine guns when necessary. Those who think that this new force of revolution is vague or unimportant are perhaps facing backward; though they think they hold the truth of the moment, they have lost the larger truth, which will always be the truth of tomorrow.

[*Combat* wants to make justice compatible with freedom]

1 October 1944

We are often asked: "What do you want?" We like this question because it is direct. We must answer it with directness. Naturally this cannot be done in only one or two articles. But by returning to the question again and again, we will give our answer clarity.

We have said many times before that what we want is to make justice compatible with freedom. It seems this is not clear enough. We shall therefore call justice a social state in which each individual starts with equal opportunity, and in which the country's majority cannot be held in abject conditions by a privileged few. And we shall call freedom a political climate in which the human being is respected both for what he is and for what he says.

All that is simple enough. The difficulty lies in maintaining a balance between the two conditions we have defined. The experience of history shows that a choice has always been made between the triumph of justice and the triumph of freedom. Only the Scandinavian democracies have come close to the desired reconciliation. Yet their example is not completely convincing because of their relative isolation and the limited range of their experiences.

Our plan is to make justice reign through the economy and to guarantee freedom through politics. Since we are staying within basic definitions, we will say that what we want for France is a collectivist economy and a liberal political structure. Without a collectivist economy to take away money's privilege and put money back to work, political liberalism would be a farce. But without the constitutional guarantee of a liberal political structure, a collectivist economy could consume all individual initiative and expression. In this delicate balance resides not human happiness, which is another matter, but the necessary and adequate conditions under which each man is solely responsible for his own happiness and his own destiny. It is simply a question of not adding human injustice to all the other profound miseries of our condition.

To sum up—and we hope we will be forgiven for saying what we have said before—we want the immediate realization of a true popular democracy. We believe that any politics separated from the working class is futile, and that the future of France is the future of its working class.

That is why we want the immediate creation of a constitution in which freedom recovers all its guarantees, and the immediate creation of an economy in which labor receives its fundamental rights. Here it is not possible to go into further detail. We will do so when it is necessary; those who have read us before know our capacity to be precise.

There are still several words to be said about method. We believe that the difficult balance we desire can be realized only in a continual state of intellectual and moral honesty, for only in such a state will we find the necessary clearsightedness. We do not believe in political realism. Dishonesty, even when well-intentioned, separates men and throws each into the most futile of solitudes. We believe, to the contrary, that men should never be isolated from one another, that in facing hard times their solidarity must be total. It is justice and freedom that fashion solidarity and reinforce communion, and justice and freedom make them genuine.

That is why we think that a political revolution must be accompanied by a moral revolution, for morality will double the power of politics and give it its true greatness. Perhaps now the reader will understand the voice we try to give to this paper. It is the voice of objectivity, open criticism, and energy. If only the effort were made to understand this voice, we believe in all sincerity that a great period of hope could begin for all France.

[*Combat* rejects anticommunism]

7 October 1944

On 26 March 1944, in Algiers, the congress of the Combat movement adopted the following principle: "Anticommunism is the beginning of dictatorship." We believe that, as we attempt to explain to our Communist comrades our position on the misunderstanding that seems to be emerging, it is important to remember this principle and to add that nothing will change it. We believe that nothing worthwhile will be accomplished without understanding. Today we would like to examine this difficult subject, using the best of our reason and humanity.

The principle set forth in Algiers was not adopted without careful consideration. The circumstances of the past twenty-five years demanded that categorical statement. This does not mean that we are Communists. But neither are those Christians who have nonetheless acknowledged a common struggle with the Communists. Our position, like that of the Christians, amounts to this: though we agree with neither the Communists' philosophy nor their practical ethics, we vigorously reject political anticommunism, for we understand both its inspiration and its tacit goals.

We thought our position firm enough to leave no room for misunderstanding. Apparently we were mistaken. We must have been careless in some of our statements, or perhaps we were simply obscure. Our task is to understand this misunderstanding and account for it. There can never be enough candor or lucidity in discussing this, one of the most important problems of the century.

Let us say plainly that a source of possible misunderstanding derives from a difference in method. We share most of our comrades' collectivist ideas and social program—specifically, their ideal of justice and their distaste for a society in which money and privilege hold first rank. But to put it simply—and our comrades will freely admit this—the Communists find, in their very coherent philosophy of history, justification for a political realism that constitutes their method for achieving what is no doubt a common ideal for many of the French people. Clearly, on this point we separate. As we have said innumerable times, we do not believe in political realism; our method is different.

Our Communist comrades can surely understand that men who do not possess as firm a doctrine as their own have had much to reflect on over the last four years. They have done this in good faith, despite a thousand perils. Among so many shattered ideals, so many innocents sacrificed, surrounded by debris and ruin, these men felt the need for both a new doctrine and a new way of life. For them, a whole world died in June 1940.

Today they search for this new truth in the same good faith and with open minds. Our Communist comrades can also understand that these men, having reflected on the bitterest of defeats, and conscious of their own shortcomings, have decided that their country has sinned by its confusion, and that henceforth the future will have meaning only through the greatest efforts of clear-sightedness and renewal.

This is the method we seek to apply today. We hope all will recognize our right to pursue it in good faith. It does not seek to change the entire politics of a country. It does seek to bring about in that country a very limited experiment with one critical objective: to introduce the language of morality into the exercise of politics. This means saying yes and no at the same time and saying them both with the same seriousness and objectivity.

Those who read us attentively, and with the simple benevolence accorded to all undertakings of good faith, might think that often what we give with one hand we seem to take away with the other. If one pays attention only to our criticisms, such misunderstanding is inevitable. But if one balances those criticisms with our much-repeated affirmations of solidarity, one can easily see that we try never to indulge in vain human passion, but always to treat justly one of the most important movements in political history.

Perhaps the intentions of our difficult method are not always obvious. Journalism is not a school of perfection. It may take a hundred issues of a newspaper to express a single idea. But this idea may clarify others, if examined with the same objectivity with which it was formulated. We may also be mistaken and our method be either utopian or impossible. But we believe this cannot be decided without giving that method a chance. This is the experiment we attempt here, as faithfully as possible, for men who have no concern other than faithfulness.

We ask our Communist comrades merely to consider this, just as we consider their own objections At the very least, we will be able to clarify our positions, and for our part, to see more clearly the difficulties and chances for our undertaking. That, at least, is what leads us to use this language—that, as well as the sense of what France would lose if, by mutual reticence and mistrust, we were driven to a political climate in which the best of the French people would refuse to live, preferring solitude to polemics and strife.

[On social order]

12 October 1944

Order is a topic frequently discussed these days. That is because order is something desirable and something we have lacked. To tell the truth, men of our generation have never known order; they have a sort of nostalgia for it that might make them incautious, were they not convinced that order must be allied with truth. This makes them a bit wary, and discriminating, regarding the various types of order proposed to them.

Order is an obscure concept; there are many different kinds. There is the order that continues to reign in Warsaw; the order that hides disorder; and the order, dear to Goethe, that stands in opposition to justice. There still exists that superior order of hearts and consciences that calls itself love, and that bloody order whereby man denies himself and that draws its power from hate. We hope to be able to discern the good order from the rest.

Today when people speak of order, they obviously mean social order. Does social order simply mean quiet in the streets? We find that unlikely, since during August's days of upheaval all of us felt that order had begun with the first shots of the insurrection. Despite their appearance of disorder, revolutions carry with them a principle of order. This principle will reign if revolution is total. But when revolution fails or is left incomplete, then widespread and continual disorder is established and remains for many years.

Can there be order without unity of government? It is certainly difficult to imagine. The German Reich achieved such unity, yet we cannot say that, as a consequence, Germany discovered its true order.

Perhaps the simple consideration of individual conduct might help us. When do we say that a man has put his life in order? It is when he has achieved an understanding of his life and conformed his conduct to what he believes to be true. The insurgent who in the disorder of passion dies for an idea he has made his own is in reality a man of order, having ordered his conduct according to a principle that was evident to him. But we will never consider a man of order the person of privilege who got three meals a day all his life, kept his fortune in secure assets, and came home whenever he heard noise in the street. He is only a man of thrift and fear. If the new order is to be one of frugality and coldness of heart, we will be tempted to hope for the worst disorder, since indifference authorizes all injustice.

We conclude that there is no order without balance and accord. Social order requires a balance between government and the governed. And accord must be made in the name of a superior principle. For us, this principle is justice. There is no order without justice; ideal order resides in a people's happiness.

Thus we cannot invoke the necessity of order to force people's wills. That would be turning the problem on its head. Not that we must have order to govern well; rather, we must govern well to achieve the only order that has any meaning. Order does not reinforce justice; justice gives its certitude to order.

No one desires as much as we do this superior order that will give us a nation at peace with itself and its destiny, where each will have his share of work and leisure, where workers can work without bitterness and envy, where the artist can create without being tormented by the sadness of man, where each will be able to reflect, in the silence of his heart, on his own condition.

We have no perverse taste for this world of violence and noise, where the best of us waste ourselves in desperate struggle. Yet we have committed ourselves to this struggle; we will see it through to the end. We want no part of an order that would consecrate our resignation and the end of human hope. That is why, deeply committed though we are to help found an order that is finally just, it must be known, too, that we are determined to reject forever the famous phrase of a false prophet and to declare that, for all eternity, we prefer disorder to injustice.[8]

[On the necessity of a new colonial politics]

13 October 1944

It would be impossible to overemphasize the importance of recent statements by the minister of colonies on the problems of the empire. Having noted the enormous role of the colonies in the Liberation movement, M. Pleven added: "The loyalty of these native peoples means for us great responsibilities. . . . A new phase of our colonial life must begin. It is a matter . . . of pursuing the conquest of hearts." Vague phrases, no doubt, yet in them we can read a purpose that is precise. M. Pleven's statements deserve further consideration.

For those of us who know colonial politics, the ignorance and indifference of the French with regard to their empire has always been a source of dismay. Once again, a small elite of administrators and adventurers have brought France a wealth that is taken for granted. But today France's position in Europe is too weak for us to forget any of our resources; we must take stock of what we have. In so doing, it would be inexcusable to ignore the lands of our empire.

But what difficult and painful problems that involves! Such problems can be solved only if we meet them head-on. "It is a matter," M. Pleven said, "of giving each colony the maximum of political personality." That is well put; the question is relatively simple when it concerns only the native populations.

But to take a specific example, if we consider the case of North Africa, we will find a French as well as a native population. As we seek to extend the political enfranchisement that the provisional government has bestowed on the natives of North Africa, we must recognize that the worst obstacle will be the French population.

It would be stupid indeed to keep from the country the fact that this French population was in large part devoted to the politics of Vichy. It was devoted to Vichy precisely because Vichy was opposed to the political enfranchisement of the native people.

What they call in North Africa, rightly or wrongly, the "colonist spirit" is always opposed to all change, even that demanded by the most basic justice. The government, to realize its politics of amity and protection toward the Algerians, must understand and reduce this resistance.

This is of the highest importance. We must not hide from ourselves the fact that, with a people as virile as the Arabs, defeat would mean for us a loss of prestige. But the French must not be tempted, in order to regain the prestige they lost by using force, to use force again. No policy could be blinder. We will find support from our colonies only when we have convinced them that their interests are our interests and that we do not have contrary policies, one giving justice to the French people, the other consecrating injustice in our empire.

These reflections have no purpose other than to underline the great difficulty of a question that involves so many national and international problems. We want it to be remembered that, above all in war, there exists a colonial problem that we must not ignore but should consider carefully and then approach with the generosity that must be ours.

[Response to Mauriac in defense of the purge]

20 October 1944

We do not agree with M. François Mauriac. We can say this without restraint since we have noted, whenever appropriate, our agreement with M. Mauriac's views.

We approve of much of his article from yesterday's *Le Figaro*. We, too, do not believe it necessary to kill our citizens on street corners or to diminish the authority of a government we have freely recognized. But these just sentiments must not lead us to depreciate our own action or renounce the most lasting of our hopes.

There certainly is a malaise in the national mood. But we do not see the same reasons for it as does M. Mauriac. Indeed, perhaps there are people in our country who know fear. Let us say only that, if they are afraid for a few months, that will be a small thing and in the long run will actually improve their welfare here on earth. But there are also others concerned with the idea that this nation has not understood that it has been betrayed by certain interests, and that it can be revived only by destroying those interests without the slightest pity.

Whatever M. Mauriac's other opinions, we part with him in his belief that this malaise, with its many and diverse causes, originates in the media about which he complains. It is true that one can see in certain newspapers both fear and indignation; perhaps certain pundits know more of these emotions than we in our ingenuousness would have supposed. But M. Mauriac uses doubtful logic in criticizing the new press first for wasting itself in quarrels, and then two articles later, for speaking as a single voice.

No, this press is not so homogeneous as M. Mauriac would suggest. He complains that it represents only the Resistance, but we tend to believe that the Resistance *is* France: what must a newspaper represent if not the resistance of the French people?

M. Mauriac's argument is that there are other things in France besides the Resistance. We do not doubt that there were times when our comrades, always faithful to their rendezvous with combat, gazed longingly at the lines in front of movie houses, or watched the motorcades of our dictators go by. But we suppose that M. Mauriac did not mean that we should take into consideration the voices of those who enjoyed themselves or who betrayed, while others offered their faces to enemy bullets.

It is not here that we will be accused of exploiting the Resistance. We repeat often enough that the Resistance has more responsibilities than rights and that tomorrow it will be judged. It is not we who will be suspected of complaisance with regard to our newspaper. We have a taste for the truth, even when it opposes us. However, we do know that yesterday the truth was not with M. Mauriac.

All is not well, it is true, in the manner in which the politics of this country is now being conducted. But one cannot ignore the fact that we sin as much through weakness as through excess. Our task is to denounce the two at the same time and to show the path whereby the force of revolution will ally itself with the light of justice. M. Mauriac speaks only of the excesses of this revolution. Our effort here is to expose at the same time its weaknesses. Our effort in itself shows that this press is not so uniform as M. Mauriac says. But that is not important. What is important is to maintain objectivity, of which M. Mauriac usually has a good sense, but which today deserts him because of his constant and honorable concern with peace at any price.

Whatever our desire and reactions may be, it is certain that France has a revolution to make at the same time as a war. It is true that this is a dramatic situation. But we will not leave this drama behind by eluding the questions it poses. We will leave it by suffering until the end and by painfully extracting from this ordeal whatever part of truth it contains. It is our conviction that there are times when we must silence our feelings and renounce our peace of mind. Ours is such a time, and its terrible law, with which it is futile to argue, forces us to destroy a living part of this country in order that we may save its very soul.

[France must both make a revolution and fight a war]

21 October 1944

Yes, the challenge for France is to make a revolution and at the same time fight a war. We are not disposed to take this lightly. There are those who would devote all to war and have justice deferred. Others would devote everything to justice before obtaining the necessary strength. But we can forget neither the strength we have to rebuild nor the purity we have to regain. And we are well aware that, in the final reality, these two must coincide. We know that the requirements of each can be mutual yet also contradictory.

How can we forget that, in both revolution and war, it is a question of French lives, the best of which will have to make themselves kill, the worst of which we will have to destroy? How can we be dispassionate in the face of a challenge that demands yet more blood from a country whose resources have been so profoundly drained by two world wars? And how can the best of us insist that there are certain hours when they have the right to add to the people's misery and to the terrible atrocity of this war?

No, we do not take this lightly; the entire world must know this. To take it lightly would mean never to doubt. It is good that from time to time we know doubt, for it provides us with the seriousness we need. We despise judges who never doubt and heroes who have never trembled.

But at the extremity of doubt there must be resolution. We are well aware that on the day the first death sentence is carried out in Paris, we will feel repugnance. But we must think then of so many other death sentences that struck innocent men, of beloved faces lying in the dust, and of hands we longed to hold. When we are tempted to prefer the generous sacrifices of war to the black chores of justice, we will have the memory of our dead and the unbearable recollection of those among us whom torture made traitors. Hard as it may be, we will know then that there are impossible pardons and necessary revolutions.

But conversely, when we have become impatient with executions that are mere public spectacles, re-established by those who should have long scorned them; when mediocrity and stupidity are once again honored and push us toward revolutions without end; when the desire to strike that sometimes seizes all men of justice makes us confuse lack of conscience with crime, then it will be time to rethink this exhausting daily task called victory. We will know that we have chosen a path toward senseless violence and inevitable war.

What does all this mean? It is to say once again that a nation which must live with such agonizing contradictions can save itself only by assuming full recognition of those contradictions, and by putting forth an enormous effort to make sure that our revolution and war cannot be separate. A great nation lifts itself up out of its own tragedies. If this country is incapable of obtaining truth at the same time as victory, if it consents to making war by permitting cowardice and treason at home, or if, on the contrary, it lets itself be swept away by the violence of its passions, neglecting its position and responsibilities in the eyes of the world, then we believe this country is lost. We will have to do everything at once or we will do nothing at all.

Is this hard, impossible, and inhuman? We know well that it is. But things are as they are, which is why we are right not to take them lightly. But our belief is that what men can imagine, they also can do. We must be neither more nor less than men. Which is to say, we must be men with hearts full of both audacity and caution, with sensible souls and firm wills, with spirits capable of both dispassion and commitment. If we are told once again that this is impossible, we will reply that that is all the more reason for attempting it, that that is why it provides our country with one last hope for greatness.

[Again replies to Mauriac that the purge is necessary]

25 October 1944

We hesitated to answer M. François Mauriac's courteous invitation in Sunday's *Le Figaro*. We thought that there were questions more urgent than these. But countless letters from our readers have convinced us that these are questions which pre-occupy many of the French people, and that we should further clarify our position.

Why not admit it? Our editorial which *Le Figaro* disputes was written with impatience. M. Mauriac's accusations had hurt us, because we had found them so profoundly unjust. Herein lies our true disagreement, and we regret that M. Mauriac passed over this question in silence. But in so doing, he unknowingly called attention to the essential problem, which of course is that of justice. Let us turn, then, to the essential.

We shocked M. Mauriac by writing that we must learn to silence our feelings. Obviously, we did not mean that we should speak counter to what we think. But it is true that the basic problem is to silence the mercifulness of which M. Mauriac speaks— for as long as truth remains in jeopardy. While it is true that this is difficult, one does not have to be a Christian to believe in the necessity of sacrifice.

Let us be precise, for it is all too easy to digress when speaking and thinking about responsibility. If we examine certain cases, for example, we may be surprised to find that the legal forms have been respected. But all this leads to confusion. We must look reality in the face; this polite discussion is carried on while heads are about to fall. Last Monday the first death sentence was

71

delivered in Paris. With this terrible fact in mind, we must take a stand. Will we or will we not approve the death penalty? This is the problem and it is a truly frightening one.

M. Mauriac will say that he is a Christian and it is not his place to condemn. But—and here we ask that M. Mauriac pay close attention—it is precisely because we are not Christians that we have decided to take on this problem and assume all its responsibilities. How?

We have no taste for murder. We respect human life more than anything in the world. Therefore our first reaction to the death penalty is repugnance. It is easy to believe that our task is simply to pursue what is good for our country, and that this does not have to involve the destruction of men. But since 1939 we have truly learned that not to destroy certain men would be to betray the good of this country. France carries within itself a diseased body, a minority of men who yesterday brought France sorrow and who continue to do so today. These are men of betrayal and injustice. Their very existence poses the problem of justice, for they constitute a living part of this country, and we must decide whether we will destroy them.

The Christian can believe that human justice is always supplemented by divine justice and consequently that indulgence is preferable. But M. Mauriac must consider the conflict of those who know no divine justice, but who nonetheless continue to believe in man and to hope to achieve his greatness. For such men the choice is between eternal silence and the pursuit of human justice. True justice will not come without upheaval. After four years of collective misery, preceded by twenty-five years of mediocrity, we can no longer doubt this. We choose human justice with all its terrible imperfections; we can hope to make it better only by holding desperately to our honesty.

We have never asked for blind or thoughtless justice. We detest capriciousness and criminal stupidity; we want to make France pure. We hope that justice will be applied swiftly and for a limited time, that the most obvious crimes will be immediately punished; then, because perfection is impossible, it will be reasonable to overlook the small mistakes made by so many of the French people.

Is this language as harsh as M. Mauriac believes? Certainly it is not the language of mercy. But it is the language of a generation of men brought up with the spectacle of injustice, men who are strangers to God but lovers of humanity, men who are resolved to serve humanity despite a destiny that is so often meaningless. It is the language of hearts determined to take charge of their responsibilities, to live with the tragedy of their century, and to serve the greatness of men in a world full of stupidity and crime.

The country's soul apparently intrigues M. Mauriac; does he know he has seen it? It was in our eyes during the marvelous days of insurrection. To keep this fire alive in the eyes of French youth, we will have to renounce that part of ourselves which would prefer the consolations of kindness and forgetting. These four years have forced us to harden something inside ourselves. Perhaps this is regrettable. Yet we see no reason why kindness cannot be strong and why firmness cannot ally itself with clemency. Come what may, this is the only chance left us to keep France and Europe from becoming a desert of mediocrity and silence where we could no longer want to live.

[France must reject concessions and complacency]

29 October 1944

The day before yesterday the minister of information gave a speech that we approve of in its entirety. But he made one point to which we must return, for a minister rarely speaks in the language of a virile morality to remind his country of its responsibilities of conscience.

M. Teitgen has succeeded in dismantling the mechanism of concession that drove so many French people from weakness to treason. Each concession made to the enemy and to the spirit of complacency led to another concession. While the second may not have been worse than the first, the two together formed an act of cowardice. Two acts of cowardice thus combined to produce dishonor.

Such is the drama of our country. And the drama is difficult to resolve, because it engages the entire human conscience. It presents the problem the cutting edge of which is whether to say yes or no.

France has lived according to a wearied "common wisdom" which told our youth that life was such that concessions had to be made; that enthusiasm belonged to the past; that in this world where might is right, one could only hope not to be wrong.

We remember how it was. When the men of our generation were startled by their first encounters with injustice, they were told they would get used to it. And thus, little by little, the morality of complacency and disillusionment was spread. We see the result: a climate that produced the trembling and disheartened voice that asked France to withdraw into itself. One can always win by addressing what comes easiest to man—his love of rest.

The love of honor, however, cannot exist without terrible demands on oneself and others. That, of course, is wearying. A certain number of French people were weary long before 1940.

But not all of them. People have expressed surprise that many of the men who joined the Resistance were not patriots by profession. First of all, patriotism is not a profession. Patriotism is a way of loving one's country that consists in never wanting that country to be unjust, and in telling it so. But patriotism itself has never been enough to make men rise to the strange struggle that is theirs. There must also be the delicacy of heart that feels repugnance at each compromise; the dignity the bourgeoisie lacks; and in a word, the capacity to say no.

The greatness of this age, so miserable otherwise, is that its choices have become pure. The refusal to compromise has become the noblest of our tasks, while the morality of concession has finally received its due contempt. Might was once right, now it is wrong. Shame, falsehood, and tyranny were once the conditions of life; now they have died.

It is the power of tenacity and dignity that today we must restore throughout French society. We must all know that each mediocrity, each surrender, each act of complacency will harm us as much as the enemy's rifles. At the end of these four years of terrible tests, a wearied France must know the extent of its drama, the fact that it no longer has the right to be weary. This is the first condition for our revival. The hope of the country is that the same men who said no will tomorrow show the same firmness and selflessness but say yes, that their honor will lead them to positive virtues as, before, it led them to their powers of refusal.

[On purity and realism]

4 November 1944

Two days ago Jean Guehenno published in *Le Figaro* a beautiful article that we could not let pass without mentioning the sympathy and respect it must inspire in all who have concern for the future of mankind. He wrote about purity—a difficult subject.

Jean Guehenno would not have taken it on himself to write about purity, had it not been for another article, intelligent but unfair, written by a young journalist who reproached Guehenno for a moral purity that the journalist believed to be no different from intellectual detachment. Jean Guehenno responded very fairly by calling for purity maintained in action.

Thus the problem of "realism" arises: we see again the question of whether or not all means are good. We are all agreed on the ends we seek, but differ in opinion on the means. All of us carry within ourselves—this we do not doubt—an unselfish passion for the impossible happiness of men. But some think one can do anything and everything to achieve that happiness, and some do not. We are among the latter. We know how quickly the means become confused with the ends; it is not just any kind of justice we seek.

This may provoke the irony of the realists, as Jean Guehenno's article has just shown. But Guehenno is right, and it is our conviction that his apparent folly is the most appropriate wisdom for our times. Indeed, this is a question of making man's salvation not in some other world, but in and through history itself. This is a question of serving the dignity of man by methods that remain dignified in the midst of a history that is not. One can imagine the difficulties and paradoxes of such an undertaking.

We know the salvation of man is perhaps impossible. But that, we insist, that is no reason to stop seeking it. Moreover, we believe no one has the right to call salvation impossible until he has spent time and effort to prove it so. The opportunity now presents itself. This country is poor and we are poor along with it. Europe is in misery and that misery is our own. With few riches and few resources, we may have been thrust into a freedom that will allow us to deliver ourselves over to the madness called truth.

We are convinced this is our final chance. We truly believe this is the last. Deception, violence, the senseless sacrifice of men— these are the means that over the centuries have proved so durable. Such proofs are bitter. There is only one thing left to try: the simple, modest path of honesty without illusion, of wise loyalty, of tenacity, which strengthens only human dignity. We believe that idealism is in vain. On the day when men put the same willfulness and untiring energy into the service of good that others have put into evil, on that day we believe the forces of good may triumph—perhaps for a very short while, but for a while nonetheless. Such victory would be unequaled.

We will no doubt be asked why we continue to dwell on this subject, when so many other questions are more urgent and more practical. But we have never hesitated to discuss practical questions; the proof is that when we have spoken out, we have not pleased everyone.

We have dwelled on this subject because no question is more urgent. Will we continue to dwell on it? Yes, so that when the world gives itself over to "realist" wisdom, and humanity returns to madness and night, men like Guehenno will remember that they are not alone and that the idea of purity, whatever others think of it, will never be forsaken.

[On the Socialist Party]

10 November 1944

The Socialist Party held the first meeting of its congress yesterday. If we can believe the reports, the party devoted itself to a rigorous self-critique. This is a promising start; we see now that it would be impossible to follow the congress's progress with too much attention. Socialist ideals are noble ones, and the Socialist Party represents one of the greatest chances for the France of tomorrow. But there is a condition: the party must make into reality the principles of renewal which it displayed yesterday at its congress.

For after all, the ideals that today capture the French imagination—justice reconciled with freedom, a collectivist economy combined with political liberalism, and the good of all based upon respect for each individual—these are Socialist ideas. If one reads carefully the basics of the programs proposed by the Christian Democrats or the National Liberation Movement, one will see that these programs could include the signature of any militant Socialist. Why is it, then, that the first impulse of men of the Resistance who belonged to no political party was not to join the Socialists?

We ask this question with complete frankness, for it is a question that many among us are now asking themselves. Let us try to answer it with equal frankness and be inspired by the courageous manner in which the Socialists asked themselves this question at their congress.

What obviously stops many from joining the Socialist Party is its past. The image we have of that past is certainly not inviting. We have known socialism to be weak and defenseless, more lavish with words than keen on action. We have known "Socialists" who are as far removed from Socialist unselfishness and self-sacrifice as certain pietists are from true Christianity. In short, we were dissuaded from joining the Socialist Party by a few of their people and by most of their methods.

While so many of socialism's sentiments and ideas are linked with our own, the Socialist Party never appeared to us to be capable of the greatness which our difficult period demands. Someone was correct to point out yesterday that the Socialists seem to have somewhat confused the goal of realizing their ideals with that of obtaining a majority in the Assembly.

Behind our criticism of socialism there was always both longing and regret: what could have been born of noble ideas led instead to meager practices; what should have been a calling was reduced to a chore. That made us lose confidence.

It would be wrong to give the impression that all our reservations have disappeared. But in the Resistance the Socialists did do their part—a large and important part—for the struggle. Today the tone they set is that of energy and courage. They seem resolved on a new faith. This resolve is of enormous importance. If the Socialists can indeed renounce the men and methods which the past has discredited or made obsolete, and if they can rebuild what should be a great party, then we are convinced that they will be the great force in tomorrow's French society, and we will unite all the efforts of the Resistance around them. But they have an enormous amount of work to do, which will be accomplished only by perseverance and lucidity. They have to defeat what is hardest of all to defeat: their habits. They will have to create a new language and make their inspiration pure once again. They have a new youth to discover. One understands the difficulty of this effort when one compares Daniel Mayer's excellent speech at the congress with Félix Gouin's address to the Assembly.[9]

We found the rhetoric of the latter regrettable. We know of not one man among us who could have been pleased or moved by hearing the Resistance praised in so pompous a fashion. We need words that are more direct and true. Let us not tire of saying this: what we need is truth and only truth. If we are so sure that M. Mayer has better understood this consuming hunger of ours, the reason is that he, at least, seems to have few bad habits to break.

In any case, the congress of the Socialist Party is an important event for all these reasons. For all those of us who are servants only to this country and to a few cherished human values, we say that we hope socialism will find among these Socialists its true expression, that it will not have to look elsewhere at the cost of yet more exhausting efforts. France needs to be served well by objective men inspired by a few clear ideas; but France also needs to be served quickly, and the best paths to achieving our renaissance are those which are short and true.

[Self-critique]

22 November 1944

It is time for a self-critique. In the profession of journalism, which consists of defining each day in the light of present circumstances, the requirements of good sense and simple honesty of spirit are constantly in jeopardy. In seeking the best, we devote ourselves to judging the worst, or sometimes only the less than best. In brief, it is easy to adopt the systematic attitude of the judge, the schoolmaster, or the professor of ethics. From our profession it is only one small step to pretension or stupidity.

We hope we have avoided that step. But we are not sure we have escaped giving the impression that we attribute to ourselves the clairvoyance and superiority of those who never make mistakes. Such is not the case. We sincerely desire to be part of a common effort to use the rules of conscience in the practice of politics; it seems to us that, until now at least, politics has not made much use of these rules.

Such is our ambition. We know, of course, when we point out the limits of other political thought and method, that our politics, too, has its limits, and that we must try scrupulously to extend those limits. But reporting daily on the events of our time is difficult; the threshold between morality and moralism is uncertain. Sometimes, out of fatigue or forgetfulness, the threshold is crossed.

How can we escape that danger? Through irony. We do not live, alas, in the age of irony. We still live in the age of indignation. But if we maintain our sense of relativity, then come what may, all can be saved.

We certainly cannot help feeling annoyed when, on the eve of the liberation of Metz,[10] knowing how much that liberation cost, we read a series of articles on Marlene Dietrich's appearance there. We have good reason to be annoyed. At the same time, this does not mean we believe newspapers have to be boring. We simply believe that in time of war the whims of a movie star are not necessarily more interesting than the suffering of people, the blood of armies, or the relentless efforts of a nation to discover its own truth.

All that is difficult. Justice is a cerebral idea and at the same time a fire in the soul. We must find the way to take from justice its human element, without transforming it into that terrible abstract passion which has led to the destruction of so many human beings. Irony is no stranger to us. It is not ourselves that we take seriously, but rather the inexpressible trial and the formidable adventure through which this country must live today. That distinction gives a sense of both measure and relativity to our daily effort.

It seems necessary to say this, and at the same time to let our readers know that in all we write, day after day, we seek to remember the careful reflection and scrupulousness that are the duty of all journalists. In our efforts of criticism, which seem so important today, we do not forget ourselves.

["Everyone in France is Socialist"]

23 November 1944

If you read the French press carefully, you will realize that everyone in France is Socialist. This is a phenomenon that we have noticed for some time. From *Le Figaro* to *Le Populaire,* the idea of a collectivist economy holds the same appeal. M. Mauriac speaks of "Socialist faith." M. Jurgensen, writing in the name of the National Liberation Movement, calls the N.L.M. a "labor movement," and the Christian Democrats describe themselves in similar terms.

This is less surprising than it may at first appear. It is not only, as is often said, that this country's inclination toward the Left is becoming more and more pronounced. It is above all that the men of the old Right have finally recognized, after four years of forced meditation, that a nation can be neither strong nor youthful if it does not assure the well-being of all its children.

But considering France's near unanimity, then, there really is something that should surprise us. For what has kept such large groups with shared opinions from uniting to form a great and independent party that would represent an overwhelming majority and be capable of bringing about, in the shortest time possible, the structural reforms essential to the rebirth of France?

The answer certainly does not lie in the religious arguments that have been discussed several times in the press. It is childish to think that the religious problem could represent an obstacle to this gathering of good wills. When the Socialists are content to remember Voltaire only for his anticlericalism, they are showing frivolity. And when M. Mauriac takes offense, he is showing his impatience too readily.

The problem of government is of such importance that we must each consider it our own problem. It is inconceivable that our situation, in which the futures of so many lives are at stake, should be compromised by the emotional arguments arising out of hearts concerned only with their own destinies.

No, it seems to us that the obstacle lies elsewhere. First of all, not everyone thinks of socialism in the same terms. What is certain is that we all feel, more or less vaguely, the urgency of the need for social justice. This already marks considerable progress. But it is still not enough; we must try to explain this political climate which is at the same time so encouraging and so troubling.

It seems to us that one can distinguish, in the different political thinking currently being expressed, two kinds of socialism: the socialism of traditional Marxist forms, represented by the Socialist Parties of the past, and a new liberal socialism, as yet to be completely formulated, but showing generosity and embraced by both groups and individuals coming from the Resistance.

This second form of socialism should have the tendency, to the extent that it can be precise in its expression, to reawaken the French collectivist tradition, which always has a place for freedom of the individual and which took nothing from philosophical materialism. This tendency is, for the moment, what seems to keep the new socialism from dissolving into its old forms.

We are witnessing, then, the confrontation of these two socialisms; our entire problem is to know if this confrontation will end in the creation of a moderate doctrine that will be that of great conciliation, or if it will lead only to a socialism that refuses to clarify itself and to express itself in a new form. We believe that France has something to gain from this confrontation. But we also believe that we should not rush into it. Instead of searching for immediate unity, we would be better off if each of us searched thoroughly for what it is he wants to unify. Socialism is not a fashion; it is a commitment. It would thus be best if everyone tried to understand the kind of commitment he is making. For example, one cannot be Socialist in principle but conservative when it comes to the economy. Socialism is for all moments and all problems.

If all those searching honestly to express the best of their aspirations are willing to put themselves to a scrupulous test, then perhaps French socialism, nourished by the energy of freedom and the permanence of justice, will finally be born, to the great joy of this nation. We should know that this hope is not a new one, and that we would only be giving form to a system of thought of which a certain Jules Guesde[11] gave several approximations.

[The new form of socialism]

24 November 1944

The more we think about it, the more we are convinced that socialist doctrine is now taking shape throughout large portions of political society. We pointed this out yesterday, but the subject deserves more attention. In the final analysis, there is nothing very original in this. Indeed, unsympathetic critics express surprise that the men of the Resistance, and so many of the French people with them, have made such enormous efforts to achieve something so thoroughly unoriginal!

First of all, it is not absolutely essential that political doctrines be new. Political thought (though not necessarily political action) can do without genius. Human affairs are complicated in detail but simple in principle. Social justice can be realized without brilliant philosophy. It requires only the basic elements of good sense, which are clearsightedness, energy, and selflessness. In these matters, to seek originality at any price would mean waiting for the year 2000. But right now—tomorrow if possible—the affairs of our society must be put in order.

Second, political doctrines do not succeed through their novelty, but through the energy and sacrifice they inspire. It is difficult to know whether theoretical socialism meant anything profound to the Socialists of the Third Republic. Today, however, socialism burns deep inside many among us. It gives form to the impatience, to the fever for justice that has so impassioned them.

Finally, perhaps because of a certain scorn for socialism, some are tempted to believe that what is now taking place is of little consequence. There is indeed a form of socialism that we hate perhaps even more than the politics of tyranny. It is the socialism that takes refuge in false optimism. It preaches love of humanity so as to exempt itself from serving men, inevitable progress so as to ignore the question of wages, and universal peace so as to avoid necessary sacrifices. That form of socialism is accomplished above all by the sacrifices of others. It was never committed to what it professed. In short, it was afraid of everything, including revolution. We have known that form of socialism all too well. It is true that its return would be of little consequence.

But there is another form of socialism, a socialism willing to make sacrifices. This socialism rejects both weakness and lies. It does not concern itself with the futile question of progress, but is convinced that the fate of men remains always in the hands of men. It does not believe in absolute and infallible doctrines, but rather in the tenacious efforts—perhaps chaotic but always untiring—to improve the human condition. For this socialism, justice is worth a revolution. And because revolution comes harder to this socialism—since it respects human lives—its revolution is all the more likely to require only the necessary sacrifices. As for knowing whether a certain disposition of heart and spirit can translate itself into accomplishments, that is a question to which we shall return.

Today we would simply like to clear up a few of the ambiguities. It is obvious that the socialism of the Third Republic never met the requirements outlined above. It now has the chance to reform. We hope it will succeed. But we also hope that the men of the Resistance, along with all French people who sympathize with them, will maintain these fundamental requirements. For if traditional socialism wants to reform itself, it will have to appeal to new men conscious of the new doctrine. It will reform itself only by adopting this doctrine and by embracing it completely. There is no socialism without the commitment and faithfulness of each of its participants. That is what we know today. And that is what is new.

[An offensive is being launched against the Resistance]

1 December 1944

The problem of the press that we mentioned yesterday [12] poses but one aspect of the offensive against the Resistance—an offensive that we had better acknowledge. While this offensive is less obvious at home than elsewhere, it is no less dangerous.

The men of the Resistance are not saints and that is good, for what France needs is not a nation of saints. The Resistance has always welcomed criticism. Here at *Combat* we have given such criticism the consideration it deserves. We have even added to that criticism when necessary, for we believe the Resistance has more responsibilities than rights. We believe further that the Resistance would lose everything, were it to become just a sect.

But what we see today is not criticism. Nor is it that effort of mutual correction by which a community together seeks a principle for progress. No, what we see is a battle on all fronts against the men and ideas that some believe to be threatening a certain order of things.

The Resistance has been ignored by many of the French people, above all by those who never did anything for it. Those who lived through the insurrection of Paris know well that the calm then reigning in the city's wealthier quarters was the calm of ignorance and indifference. The men who did not want the world to change, since it had so favored them, thought that the Resistance was simply a group of French patriots who had mobilized themselves for a short period of time. They were inclined to condescending smiles.

The Resistance was in fact what they thought. But then it became something more. It became a force for renovation that conceived the idea of a just France as it forged the reality of a free France. The men who do not want the world to change feel today that they were mistaken. The liberation of France had meant for them merely a return to their traditional meals, their family cars, and *Paris-Soir*. Let liberation come quickly so that we can return to our mediocrity and comfort!

But the Resistance insists that we must not rest, that we have much more to accomplish, and that combat continues. The Resistance insists that we must accept being poor so that the country can be rich, that we must consent to deprivations so that the people finally receive what is necessary. And in the end the Resistance calls itself socialist. There has been a misunderstanding.

It is by means of this misunderstanding that they will try to make the Resistance pay. People want to rest, to keep their privileges: the offensive has begun. All we can do is accept the struggle. But their timing is good. We are growing weary of these continual attacks against what they call a fraction of the country, forgetting how much the country owes that "fraction."

The Resistance is growing tired of hearing that it does too much today and will not do enough tomorrow, that it is but one group isolated from the rest of society, that it is beginning to collapse under the weight of its own divisions.

Thus far the Resistance has received this criticism gracefully, with both an admirable desire for objectivity and a youthful lack of pretentiousness. The Resistance has been disposed to forgive mediocrity and self-interest. It would be enough if the former did not assert itself too aggressively, and if the latter realized that it was in the best interest of self-interest to keep quiet and concede what it must. That we could accept, for we are not as eager for destruction as is suggested in certain quarters. On the contrary, when one passionately desires unity, one resigns oneself to a certain amount of mediocrity and cupidity, knowing just how pervasive they are. But when the greedy show themselves to be so blind and obstinate as to attempt to harm the struggle, when they stupidly try to stop what can no longer be stopped, then they must be crushed—not because of any abstract principle, but because we must continue our work.

That is what the Resistance is beginning to understand. Perhaps it is salutary that the men on the other side are doing so much to help them attain this understanding. They help us to remember that, after four years of madly longing for freedom and justice, we cannot through our mercy forget the revolution we must make.

One statesman who had a good idea of what a revolution is, said on the day following a great political success: "First, do not sing victory. Second, annihilate the enemy, for he is neither beaten nor destroyed. Third, do not boast until your goals have been achieved—but then, of course, boasting will no longer be necessary."

We know today that the enemy must be destroyed. We know that our goal is the victory that comes without having to be sung.

Part II

THE REVOLUTION RUINED: TOWARD A THIRD WAY

[Quotes Edgar Quinet[13] on how to ruin a revolution]

17 December 1944

Once a revolution has broken out, what must you do to ruin it? Experience shows that you should first applaud it; above all, praise the generosity, the selflessness, the magnanimity of the people. If the people begin to assert themselves, then the time has come to proclaim, with all the mouths at your disposal, that the revolution must not be dishonored, that to try to take advantage of it would be to tarnish the victory, that the satisfaction of revolution comes in having finished it, but that trying to guarantee all the revolution's promises might very well diminish the revolution's glory.

When you have thus put the people to sleep with endless praise of their unselfishness, you can then go even further. You must make them think the weapons they hold are a sign of disorder; they could present a dazzling example of wisdom by giving the weapons to designated individuals or to a special corps that would be instituted to bear the weapons in the people's place.

As soon as the people are disarmed, you must once again praise them: tell them that their strength and nobility remind you of a kind-hearted lion! But the very next day you should insinuate that the revolution everyone thought so pure was not without its various crimes, that there were madmen mixed among the heroes. But happily, the evil ones were in the minority.

The following day you will be able to remove all your restraints. And if nothing seems in jeopardy, the moment has come to announce that this revolution, which at first glance seemed so promising, was after all nothing but a criminal act, that its only motivation lay in pilferage, but that—thank God!—we have all escaped the wickedness of its principles. Indeed, the people have witnessed enough ruin, thefts, murders, incendiaries, and infamies to know what the revolution would have led to, had it not been crushed in its infancy.

Once you have said this, experience shows you that you cannot repeat it too often, until the people, blinded by so many sudden accusations, will finally believe that they really did escape from an abyss of wickedness. Now is the moment to profit from their fear, which will soon turn into stupor, creeping up from behind to put the bridle on revolution's victory.

Thus spoke Edgar Quinet in 1868. We see that little has changed in this world. One can read even in the Greek histories how the aristocrats of certain Hellenic cities, in order to manipulate their peoples, used such rhetoric. To this principle, two thousand years old, corresponds the method that Quinet defined and that we see demonstrated today. We have had with us for centuries, then, speeches which have never been finished but will always continue.

[The tragedy of separation]

22 December 1944

France has lived through many tragedies that have now been concluded. France will live through many more tragedies that have not yet begun. But there is one tragedy through which the men and women of this country have continually suffered these past five years: the tragedy of separation.

One's homeland far away. Lovers cut off from each other. The conversations with shadows that somehow sustain two human beings across the plains and mountains of Europe, or the futile monologues that each pursues while awaiting the other. These are the miserable signs of our age. For five years French men and women have waited. For five years in their deprived hearts they have struggled desperately against time, against the thought of their absent loved ones growing older and of all the years for happiness and love that have been lost.

Yes, this is the age of separation. Who would dare speak the word "happiness" in these tortured times? Yet millions today continue to seek happiness. These years have been for them only a prolonged postponement, at the end of which they hope to find that the possibility for happiness has been renewed. Who could blame them? And who could say that they are wrong? What would justice be without the chance for happiness? What purpose would freedom serve, if we had to live in misery? We French know these questions well. We entered this war not because of any love of conquest, but to defend a certain notion of happiness. Our desire for happiness was so fierce and pure that it seemed to justify all the years of unhappiness. Let us retain the memory of that happiness and of those who have lost it. That will alleviate the loneliness of our struggle and add courage to the sadness of France and to the tragedy of France's separated children.

I will not write here what I really think of separation. This is neither the place nor the time to write that, for me, separation seems the rule and reunion the exception. Happiness is a prolonged risk; what all of us await are words of hope. Our generation has always striven toward one goal: to rise above despair. Perhaps that has prepared us to speak of the great search for hope that continues despite the world's misery. The search is in itself a kind of victory. Optimism now seems to us the only worthy course. There is only one thing we cannot triumph over—the eternal separation that ends all. As for the rest, there is nothing that cannot be faced with courage and love. Courage and love maintained for five years is the inhuman test imposed on the men and women of France. Such is the measure of their suffering.

That is what we commemorate in this Week of the Absent. One week is not very long. Why does it often seem easier to be ingenious in the pursuit of evil than in the pursuit of good? We want to relieve misery but have few methods to do so. So we give money. I hope we will give a lot. We can do little for pain; let us at least do something for poverty. The pain may be somewhat alleviated, and at least some of these frustrated, suffering people will be able to afford the rent. For many, that would be a luxury they have done without for a long time.

So that no one will think himself absolved, however, so that money alone will not give clean consciences, let us remember some debts are inexhaustible. To all those men and women far away, to that immense, mysterious, and fraternal crowd, we will give the faces of those whom we love and who have been torn from us. We know all too well that in those moments when they turned to us, we neither loved nor appreciated them nearly enough. No one loved them enough, not even their country, which is why they are where they are today. This week, *our* week, must not allow us to forget *their* years. It must teach us to love them with more than a mediocre love; it must help us find the memory and imagination that will make us worthy of them. Above all, this week must help us forget the vainest of our words, and prepare the silence that we will offer our loved ones on the difficult and magnificent day when they are once again before us.

[Criticism of the pope for not having condemned dictatorship earlier]

26 December 1944

The pope has just delivered a message to the world in which he openly endorses democracy. We welcome this. But we also believe that this carefully nuanced message deserves an equally nuanced response. We are not sure that this response will express the opinion of all our comrades in the Combat movement, among whom are many Christians. But we are sure that it will convey the feelings of a great many among us.

Since the opportunity has presented itself, we would like to note that our satisfaction with the pope's message is not entirely free from regret. For years now we have been waiting for the greatest spiritual authority of our times to condemn in clear terms the ventures of dictatorships. I repeat: in clear terms. For this condemnation may be found in certain encyclical letters, if they are read and correctly interpreted. But these letters and the language in which they are written have never been very accessible to the vast majority of men.

This great majority have waited all these years for a voice to raise itself and clearly state, as it did today, where evil lies. Our secret wish is that it had spoken out when evil was triumphant and the forces opposing evil had been silenced. That the Church speaks now, as the spirit of dictatorship is waning, is obviously cause for rejoicing. But we do not want simply to rejoice. We want to believe and admire. We want spirit to prove itself instead of being asserted and proven right by force.

We, like Georges Bernanos,[14] would have preferred this repudiation of Franco in 1936. The voice that has just told the Catholic world which side to take was the only voice that could have spoken in the midst of torture and screams, the only voice that could deny, calmly and fearlessly, the blind force of armies.

Let us state clearly that we wanted the pope to assume his responsibility during those shameful years and denounce what had to be denounced. It is difficult to accept the fact that the Church left this responsibility to those in obscurity, to those who lacked its authority, to those deprived of the invincible hope by which the Church lives. The Church did not have to be preoccupied with self-preservation. Even in chains, the Church never ceases to exist. The Church could have claimed a strength that today we do not recognize the Church as having.

Now, at least, the message we awaited has been delivered. Catholics who gave the best of themselves in our common struggle now know that they were right, that they were on the side of good. The virtues of democracy have been recognized by the pope. But it is here that nuance begins. The pope understands democracy in its broadest sense; he says that it includes monarchies as well as republics. This democracy distrusts the masses, whom Pius XII subtly distinguishes from the people. This democracy accepts social inequalities; it merely tempers them by the spirit of fraternity.

Democracy, as defined in this text, has paradoxically a radical-socialist nuance, which does not fail to surprise us. As for the rest, the decisive word has been spoken; the pope has made clear his desire for a politics of moderation.

We can certainly understand this desire. There is a moderation of spirit that adds to the intelligence of social undertakings as well as to the general happiness of men. Yet so much nuance and caution give license to the kind of moderation that is most hateful of all—moderation of the heart. That kind of moderation permits inequality and suffers the continuation of injustice.

The advocacy of moderation is double-edged. It risks serving those who want to conserve everything, those who have failed to understand that some things must be changed. Our world does not need tepid souls. It needs burning hearts that know how to put moderation in its proper place. The Christians of the first century were not moderates. Today the Church has the duty of not allowing itself to be confused with the forces of conservatism.

We say this because we believe that those who aspire to name and honor in this world must serve the cause of freedom and justice. In this struggle we can never say too much; that is why, at times, we can afford to speak cautiously. Indeed, who are we to dare criticize the highest spiritual authority of the century? We are nothing, really, mere defenders of the spirit who will never forget their duty toward those whose mission it is to represent the spirit.

[The purge has gone awry]

5 January 1945

The press seems preoccupied with injustice these days, because there is no justice to write about. A Roman Catholic wrote
that there was justice only in hell. Our courts are doing everything they can to prove this unfortunate statement true. News-
writers and editorialists thus have to choose between writing
about absurd condemnations and ridiculous acts of forgiveness.
Meanwhile prisoners are dragged out of their cells and shot because they have been pardoned.

We would like to say only that all this is in the order of things,
and that now it is probably too late for justice to be done. What
we wished for was difficult to achieve, because we had to reconcile the hard necessity of pitilessly destroying those who had betrayed us with concern that we might lose the respect owed to the
individual. That was why justice had to be done quickly.

We are told now that this was never possible, that several weeks
were not enough to find the betrayers, judge, and punish them.
But we know that well; it was never the real problem. The real
problem, so that justice could be done quickly, was to make justice clear. We must explain ourselves here, for we have obviously
not been understood.

For a defeated country, treason sometimes weighs more heavily on the conscience of those who were betrayed than on those
who committed the betrayals. For those who were betrayed must
then think of punishing. This ugly word has always been repugnant to delicate hearts. Nonetheless, we had to accept the idea of
punishment, put it in the service of human justice, and destroy
those who had destroyed. And if this task was not already sufficiently difficult and discouraging, there was also the problem of

performing it scrupulously, which meant performing it according to the law. Now we must say this well and often: there is no law which can be applied to the form of treason we have all experienced. The problem that we have to resolve is a problem of conscience, which takes form essentially in a law that has never been written. We live in a world in which one can lose honor without ceasing to be respected by the law.

What was there to do, then, if not to create the law we lacked? But here again our scruples stopped us. For the law we needed would have to be applied to offenses created before the law's creation. And we knew that making laws retroactively is the mark of all repressive regimes and dictatorships.

So was it necessary to accept our impotence, to use only the laws at our disposal, which of course could do nothing? It seems as if that is exactly what we have done. The results are there. They are what make us feel justified in saying that it was necessary to go to the end of our contradiction, to accept resolutely that we would appear unjust in order to serve justice truly. There is no need to mention how the friends of those who are judged today would settle the matter, if they ever returned to Paris as masters. But that does not matter. What did matter was the creation of a law we need, and the formulation of that law in clear and irreproachable terms. What mattered, finally, in order that we might compensate for the law's retroaction, was to assign the law a precise time limit, past which it would no longer be valid. Five months ago, it was possible to act because it had become possible to speak clearly. True, the government could not have arrested all those guilty within a few weeks. But they could have, within a few weeks, created a law of honor which would have lasted six months or a year, and which would have cleansed France of the shame which still exists today.

But now it is too late. We will condemn to death still more journalists who never deserved anything like the death penalty.

We will acquit more officials simply because they were capable of speaking well on their own behalf. And the people, weary of such impotent justice, will continue from time to time to take justice into their own hands. A certain good natural sense will keep us from the worst excesses; but fatigue and indifference will do the rest. People get used to everything, even shame and stupidity. And where could they ask for more shame and stupidity than from their Ministry of Justice?

All this is, in effect, in the order of things. But we do not say this without bitterness and sadness. A country which forgoes self-purgation must be prepared to lose its rebirth. Nations have the face that their justice brings them. We wish we had something to show the world besides a dissolute face. But clarity and hard, human virtue do not come by themselves. For lack of them, we are going to need vain consolations. We see now that M. Mauriac was right: we are going to need charity.

Justice and Charity

11 January 1945

M. Mauriac has just printed an article with the title "In Contempt of Charity," an article which I find neither just nor charitable. For the first time in the issues that separate us, he has written in a tone which I will not emphasize here but which I, at least, have always refused to take. Moreover, I would not have answered, if circumstances were not forcing me to leave these daily debates, in which the best and the worst of us have spoken over these past months, never shedding light on any of the things that matter to us. I would not have answered if I did not feel that this discussion, of which the subject is our very lives, was starting to turn to complete confusion. And since M. Mauriac's article addresses me personally, I would like to speak in my own name and try one last time to make clear what I have always wanted to say, and then be finished with the subject.

Each time the purge has been discussed, I have spoken of justice while M. Mauriac has spoken of charity. And the virtue of charity is so unassailable that when I demand justice, I seem to be asking for hate. To listen to M. Mauriac, one would really think that in daily affairs the choice is between the love of Christ and the hate of man. It is not! We refuse both the cries of hate that come at us from one side and the pleas of mercy that come at us from the other. Somewhere between the two, we look for the just voice that will give us truth without shame. To find that voice, we do not need clarity on every point; but we do need to strive continuously toward clarity with the passion that comes from intelligence and from the heart, and without which neither M. Mauriac nor ourselves would ever do anything of value.

This is what enables me to say that charity has no place here. In this respect, I have the impression that M. Mauriac has not read carefully the texts he tries to contradict. I understand that he is a writer of wit and not of reason, but I would prefer that we speak without humor in these matters. For M. Mauriac has badly misunderstood me, if he thinks I recommend smiling at the world that has been offered us. When I say that the charity which M. Mauriac proposes is a vain consolation for the masses starved for justice, I hope he knows that I say this, too, without smiling.

As much as I respect M. Mauriac, I have the right to disagree with him. He does not have to respond as he has done, by so generously attributing to me contempt for charity! No, both our positions should be made clear. M. Mauriac does not want to add to hate, and in this I will gladly follow him. But I do not want to add to lies, and in that I expect him to follow me. In short, I expect him to say that there still exists a need for justice.

In truth, I do not believe he will do it; it is a responsibility he refuses to take. M. Mauriac, who has written that our Republic should be strong, seems to be on the verge of writing a word that he has not yet spoken: pardon. I will say only that I see two paths that lead to the death of our country (and there are ways to survive that would be no better than death). The two paths are those of hate and pardon. Each seems to me as disastrous as the other. I have no taste for hate. The very idea of hating is to me the most wearisome in the world; it took every effort for my comrades and me to endure this idea. But forgiveness does not seem any better, and today it would come as an insult. In any case, my conviction is that forgiveness is not within our realm of possibilities. Though I may detest the death sentence, my feelings are not the only ones involved: I will join M. Mauriac in openly forgiving, only when the parents of Vélin and the wife of Leynaud tell me I can.[15] But not before; no, never before, lest, for the mere sake of pouring out my heart, I betray that which I have always loved and respected in this world, that which makes the nobility of man, that which constitutes faithfulness.

This is perhaps difficult to hear. I hope only that M. Mauriac realizes that it is no less difficult to say. I wrote plainly that Béraud[16] did not deserve death. But I do not have enough imagination to believe, as M. Mauriac does, that having created treason is in itself a heavy enough burden to bear. Indeed, we need all our imagination for those Frenchmen who for four years were on the side of honor; we have none to spare for the journalists now being made into martyrs whenever they are rightly found guilty. As a man, I can perhaps admire M. Mauriac for knowing how to love traitors; but as a citizen, I deplore it, for this love will turn us into a nation of betrayal and mediocrity, of which we have already had quite enough.

Finally, M. Mauriac has concluded by throwing Christ in my face. I would like in all seriousness to say only this: I believe I well understand the greatness of Christianity; but we are among those in this tormented world who believe that Christ may have died to save others, but that he did not die to save us. At the same time, we refuse to lose hope for man. We do not have the unrealistic ambition of saving him; we try only to serve him. If we consent to dispense with God and hope, we do not dispense so easily with man. On this point, I can tell M. Mauriac with confidence that we will not be discouraged, that we will forever refuse a divine charity which frustrates the justice of men.

[Reviews and confirms *Combat*'s position]

9 February 1945

It may seem as if *Combat* has changed its direction, as if it has been seized by the fever of opposition. It is true that since the Liberation many things and many people have changed. I suppose that is the reason for accusations of inconstancy against those who have always remained committed to what they have said.

In any case, I must affirm that *Combat* has never changed its position. Our staff has always remained united; we maintained our unity in the midst of the insurrection, and we maintain it now in the midst of great confusion. The editorialists of this paper answer to one another.

Those who have read us attentively know it well. We have always said that liberation does not mean freedom, that the combat against the Nazi enemy could not confuse us about the fight against moneyed privileges. We have never stopped asserting that the international system of alliances would not suffice, and that our only hope was a world organization which would finally assure peace among peoples.

For six months we have defended the same program without ever straying from it. For six months we have demanded an economy for war and for reconstruction; we have demanded socializations (first of all, of credit) which would put production in the service of the collectivity, instead of abandoning production to the private interests whose resignations we have already accepted. For six months we have demanded the creation of a true popular democracy with a just economy and a liberal political principle. For six months we have been conscious of the contradiction which strangles a world caught between an inevitably international economy and obstinately nationalistic policies; we have therefore demanded a world economic federation, whose first concerns would be the internationalization of commercial markets and of currency, thus preparing a political federation that will keep the peoples of this world from cutting each others' throats every twenty years.

Last August we were not so alone in defending this program, nor were we so original. Indeed there was near unanimity, which made our hopes great. The government had accepted the program's principles. And that is precisely why we supported the government, though still maintaining our vigilance and trying to defend the common hope with the language of objectivity. What is it, then, that has changed, to the surprise of some of our comrades? Let us say without hesitation that what has changed is not our convictions, but rather the intentions of our government.

The decisions taken these past weeks, the policies of certain ministers, contradict the program. There are ministers who no longer have our support because they no longer have our approval. It is not we who today isolate ourselves; it is the government. For we are not so alone. The Socialist Party, the labor unions, and finally the C.N.R. have joined in supporting this program. Even M. Cachin [17] himself, in two successive articles, has just changed the last declarations of the Communist Party and has joined us in demanding the necessary socializations. No, nothing has changed—except perhaps the government's goals.

What more is there to say? The word "opposition" has been applied to us. I personally find it unfortunate; I wish it could be avoided. But we will choose it tomorrow without hesitation, if the announced national program shows that the government has not kept its promises. For we also have our promises to keep. We made them at a time when humiliation had become our national religion and resignation our national politics. We will stay faithful to our promise for our own sake and for the sake of this nation's people. After all, among our promises was that of integrity, and we shall keep it.

[Demands the release of prisoners still in Dachau[18]]

17 May 1945

"For food we have a bowl of soup at noon, and coffee with a bit of bread in the evening. . . . We are covered with fleas and lice. . . . Every day Jews die. Their corpses are piled in a corner of the camp until the pile is considered big enough to be buried. . . . Meanwhile, during the long hours and days, and under a hot sun, a sickening odor spreads throughout the Jewish camp and into our own."

The camp filled with the terrifying smell of death is Dachau. We have known of it for a long time, and the world begins to grow weary of so many atrocities. The fastidious will find this monotonous and reproach us for speaking of it again. But France will perhaps find new sensitivity, when it learns that this cry comes from one of thousands of political prisoners in Dachau eight days after its liberation by American troops. These men have been kept in their camps waiting for a repatriation that they do not see coming. In the same place where they thought they had experienced the extremities of anguish, they today know even greater suffering, for now they have been deprived of the confidence that kept them going.

The extracts we cited are taken from a four-page letter from a prisoner to his family. We present these extracts for the enlightenment of all. A great deal of evidence led us to believe that conditions were such for our deported comrades. But we refrained from speaking of the subject until we had obtained more certain information. Today this is no longer possible: the first message to reach us from Dachau is proof and now we must shout our indignation and anger. It is a disgrace which must be stopped.

It is indeed a disgrace that the German troops have abundant food and supplies and Hitler's officers dine as usual, while political prisoners go hungry. It is a disgrace that while the famous deportees ["*déportés d'honneur*'"] are repatriated immediately and by airplane, our comrades still know the same hopeless surroundings that they have been forced to contemplate for years. These men do not ask much. They do not want special treatment. They demand neither medals nor speeches. They simply want to go home. They have had enough. They were willing to suffer to achieve the Liberation; but they cannot understand why they must suffer in spite of it. Yes, they have had enough, for they have suffered terribly for this victory, which is truly, and in a way that this world indifferent to the spirit cannot understand, *their* victory.

It must be known that a single hair from the head of one of these men is more important to France and to the rest of the world than a dozen of the politicians whom photographs always show smiling. These comrades alone have been the guardians of honor and the witnesses of courage. This is why we must declare that, if we cannot tolerate their living in the midst of hunger and disease, surely we cannot tolerate their also being forced to despair.

In his letter, of which each line should provoke the reader's fury and revolt, our comrade speaks of V-day at Dachau: "No shouts, no displays; that day brought us nothing." Can it be understood what this means when it is a matter of men who, instead of waiting for victory to come from the other side of the sea, sacrificed everything to hasten the day of their most cherished hope? And now that day is here! It finds them in the midst of corpses and stench, trapped by barbed wire, excluded from a world which in their darkest moments they never imagined to be so stupid and oblivious.

We will stop here. But if our cries are ignored, if immediate measures are not announced by Allied organizations, we will repeat our call; we will employ all methods at our disposal to shout across all borders, to let the world know the lot accorded by victorious democracies to witnesses who have sacrificed themselves so that the democracies' principles would have at least a chance at truth.

[On the bombing of Hiroshima]

8 August 1945

The world is what it is, which is to say, nothing much. That is what everyone learned yesterday, thanks to the formidable concert of opinion coming from radios, newspapers, and information agencies.[19] Indeed we are told, in the midst of hundreds of enthusiastic commentaries, that any average city can be wiped out by a bomb the size of a football. American, English, and French newspapers are filled with eloquent essays on the future, the past, the inventors, the cost, the peaceful incentives, the military advantages, and even the life-of-its-own character of the atom bomb.

We can sum it up in one sentence: our technical civilization has just reached its greatest level of savagery. We will have to choose, in the more or less near future, between collective suicide and the intelligent use of our scientific conquests.

Meanwhile we think there is something indecent in celebrating a discovery whose use has caused the most formidable rage of destruction ever known to man. What will it bring to a world already given over to all the convulsions of violence, incapable of any control, indifferent to justice and the simple happiness of men—a world where science devotes itself to organized murder? No one but the most unrelenting idealists would dare to wonder.

These discoveries must be reported and given appropriate commentary; they must be announced to the world so that man has an accurate picture of his destiny. But couching these terrible revelations in picturesque or humorous writing is intolerable.

Even before the bomb, one did not breathe too easily in this tortured world. Now we are given a new source of anguish; it has all the promise of being our greatest anguish ever. There can be no doubt that humanity is being offered its last chance. Perhaps this is an occasion for the newspapers to print a special edition. More likely, it should be cause for a certain amount of reflection and a great deal of silence.

For the rest, there are other reasons to be skeptical about the optimistic stories that the media offer us. When one sees that the foreign affairs editor of Reuters has announced that this invention makes the treaties of Potsdam void and outdated, while remarking that he is indifferent to the Russians' presence in Königsberg or to the Turks' in the Dardanelles, one cannot help but suspect that this beautiful concert of opinions is quite removed from scientific impartiality.

Let us be understood. If the Japanese surrender after the destruction of Hiroshima, having been intimidated, we will rejoice. But we refuse to see anything in such grave news other than the need to argue more energetically in favor of a true international society, in which the great powers will not have superior rights over small and middle-sized nations, where such an ultimate weapon will be controlled by human intelligence rather than by the appetites and doctrines of various states.

Before the terrifying prospects now available to humanity, we see even more clearly that peace is the only goal worth struggling for. This is no longer a prayer but a demand to be made by all peoples to their governments—a demand to choose definitively between hell and reason.

[The purge is a failure and a disgrace]

30 August 1945

Excuse us for starting today with an obvious truth: it is now certain that the purge in France is not only a failure but also a disgrace. The word *purge* is painful enough in itself. That which it describes has become hateful. It could have succeeded only if undertaken without vengeance or frivolity. Obviously, the road to simple justice was difficult to follow, with the screams of hate on one side and the pleadings of bad conscience on the other. In any case, the failure is complete.

But it is just as well that politics, with all its blindness, should have such extremes to check each other. Too many have demanded the death penalty, as if forced labor, for example, were not adequate punishment. But on the other hand, too many have shouted in terror when a few years were given for the crime of denunciation and dishonor. Either way we are powerless. Perhaps the most obvious course of action now is to do what we must, so that flagrant injustice does not further poison the air which the French already find hard to breathe.

There is a particular injustice that we would like to speak of today. The same court that condemned Albertini, a recruiting officer for the L.V.F.,[20] to five years of forced labor, condemned the pacifist René Gérin, who wrote the literary column for *L'Oeuvre*[21] during the war, to eight years of forced labor. Neither logic nor justice can justify that. We are not expressing approval for René Gérin. Total pacifism seems to us to be poorly reasoned, for we know that there always comes a time when it is no longer tenable. Nor can we condone that Gérin wrote, albeit only on literary subjects, for *L'Oeuvre*.

However, we must respect proportion and judge men according to what they are. Forced labor is not appropriate punishment for a few literary articles, even if written for an Occupation newspaper. Moreover, Gérin's position never changed. One may not share his point of view but still see that his pacifism was at least the result of a certain conception of man that can only be respected. A society condemns itself when it shows itself incapable, for want of definition or clear ideas, of punishing real criminals, and instead sends to penal servitude a man who only by accident found himself in the company of false pacifists who loved not peace but Hitler. Cannot a society that wants and aspires to a rebirth at least have a basic concern for clarity and distinction?

Gérin denounced no one and participated in no enemy activities. If it is determined that his literary collaboration with *L'Oeuvre* deserves punishment, then punishment should be imposed, but in proportion to the offense. The penalty of forced labor is so excessive that it makes up for nothing. Instead, it arouses the suspicion that such a judgment is that of a class and not a nation. It humiliates a man for no reason and to no one's benefit. It discredits a policy to the harm of all.

In any case, this process must be changed—not only to stop a man from suffering a penalty disproportionate to his errors, but so that justice itself can be maintained and be, at least in one case, respectable. Even if René Gérin was in a camp other than our own, it seems to us that here all independent opinion must be with us, if we are to salvage anything in the realm of justice.[22]

Part III

"NEITHER VICTIMS NOR EXECUTIONERS"

The Century of Fear

19 November 1946

The seventeenth century was the century of mathematics, the eighteenth that of the physical sciences, and the nineteenth that of biology. Our twentieth century is the century of fear. I will be told that fear is not a science. But science is no doubt involved, for its latest advances have brought it to the point of negating itself, while its perfected technology threatens the entire world with destruction. Moreover, if fear itself cannot be considered a science, it is certainly a technique.

What is indeed most striking about our world is that most men (with the exception of true believers) are cut off from the future. Life has no validity unless it projects itself toward the future, unless it promises growth and progress. Living with one's back to the wall is a life for dogs. Well, the men of my generation, those who today enter factories and universities, are living more and more like dogs.

Of course this is not the first time that men have found themselves before a future substantially closed to them. But before, they could still triumph through words and protest. They could appeal to other values which gave them hope. Today nobody speaks anymore (except those who repeat themselves), because the world seems to be in the grip of deaf and blind forces that heed neither cries of warning and advice nor cries for help. The spectacle of these years has destroyed something in us. It has finally repressed the once irrepressible confidence which man had in himself, that he could inspire in other men human reactions simply by speaking the language of humanity. We have seen men lie, dishonor, deport, torture; they could not be persuaded to stop because they were so sure of themselves, because it is not possible to persuade an abstraction—that is, the representative of an ideology.

The long dialogue among men has just come to an end. Naturally, a man who will not listen is a man to be feared. And so, along with those who have not spoken because they thought it useless, a vast conspiracy of silence has spread among us, a conspiracy sustained by those whose interests reside in silence. "You must not speak of the cultural purge in Russia or you will help reaction." "You must keep quiet about the Anglo-American support of Franco or you will encourage communism." I was right when I said that fear is a technique.

What with the general fear of a war for which all the world is now preparing, and the specific fear of murderous ideologies, it is really true that we all live in terror. We live in terror because dialogue is no longer possible, because man has surrendered entirely to history, because he can no longer find that part of himself, every bit as real as history, that sees beauty in the world and in human faces. We live in a world of abstractions, bureaucracies and machines, absolute ideas, and crude messianism. We suffocate among people who think they are right in their machines as well as in their ideas. For those who can live only with dialogue, only with the friendship of men, this silence means the end of the world.

If we are to emerge from this terror, we need to reflect, then act upon reflection. But an atmosphere of terror hardly encourages reflection. Nonetheless, my opinion is that fear should not be used as an excuse; we must recognize fear as the basic element of our situation and then try to change it. No task is more important. For it involves the fate of a vast number of Europeans who have been overwhelmed by violence and lies and deprived of their greatest hopes. Repelled by the idea of killing their fellow human beings in the name of persuasion, they find equally distasteful the idea of themselves being "persuaded" in the same manner! Yet such is the alternative for so many of us in Europe who belong to no political party, or who are ill at ease in the party they have chosen, who doubt that socialism will be realized in Russia or liberalism in America, but who nonetheless recognize that each has the right to affirm its truth, but refuse each the right to impose its truth by individual or collective murder. Among the powerful today, these are men without kingdoms. They will not make their position recognized (and I say recognized, not triumphant), nor will they recover their kingdom, until they know precisely what they want and proclaim it simply and loudly enough to make their words inspire action. And if fear does not create an atmosphere for careful reflection, then they will have to learn to conquer fear.

To conquer fear, we must understand what fear implies and what it rejects. The paradox is that it implies and rejects the same thing: a world where murder is legitimate and where human life is considered trifling. This is the essential political problem of our day; before we worry about the rest, we must first answer two questions. Do you or do you not, directly or indirectly, want to be killed or be a victim of violence? Do you or do you not, directly or indirectly, want to kill or commit violence? All those who answer no to both questions are automatically committed to a series of consequences which will change the way

in which these questions are posed. I will consider in the following articles two or three of these consequences. While awaiting
my next article, the reader should think about these questions
and try to answer them.

To Save Lives

20 November 1946

I once said that, after the experiences of the past two years,
I could no longer hold to any truth that might oblige me, directly
or indirectly, to condemn a man to death. Certain thoughtful
people whose opinions I usually respect replied that I was dream-
ing of a utopia, that political truths must eventually choose the
extremity of murder or else fail to change the world.

They argued their point most forcefully. But I think that they
were able to argue with such force because they refused to imagine other people's deaths. It is a peculiarity of our times. We
make love by telephone, we no longer work with material but
with machines, and we kill and are killed by proxy. We gain in
neatness but lose in understanding.

Yet their argument has another strength, albeit indirect: it
poses the problem of utopia. People like myself want not a world
where murder no longer exists (we are not so crazy as that!), but
one where murder is no longer legitimized. Here we are indeed
utopian—and contradictorily so. For we live in a world where
murder is legitimized, and if we do not like that, we must change
it. But it seems we cannot change it without running the risk

of murder. Murder thus brings us back to murder, and we will continue to live in terror whether we accept it with resignation or suppress it with means that substitute one form of terror for another.

I believe that everyone should think this over carefully. What strikes me in the midst of polemics, threats, and outbursts of violence is the good will of all. Everyone from Right to Left, except only a few hypocrites, believes that his truth is the one that will bring happiness to men. Yet all this good will has produced this infernal world where men are still killed, threatened, and deported, where war is prepared, where one cannot speak freely without being immediately insulted or betrayed. Thus if people like ourselves live in contradiction, we are not the only ones, and those who accuse us of being utopian no doubt have utopias of their own which are, in the end, more costly than ours.

We must admit, then, that the refusal to legitimize murder forces us to reconsider our whole idea of utopia. This much seems clear: utopia is that which is in contradiction with reality. From this point of view, we would have to be completely utopian to believe that men would no longer kill other men. There would be absolute utopia. But in a more relative utopia we could demand that murder be no longer legitimized. Indeed, Marxist and capitalist ideologies, both based on the idea of progress, both convinced that the application of their principles will inevitably lead to a harmonious society, are utopian to a far greater degree. Moreover, they both cost us dearly.

We can therefore conclude that in the next few years the struggle will not be between utopia and reality, but between different utopias, each trying to impose itself on reality. It will no longer be a matter of choosing the least costly among them. My conviction is that we can no longer hope to save everything, but that we can at least try to save lives, so that some kind of future, if perhaps not the ideal one, will remain possible.

The refusal to legitimize murder, then, is no more utopian than the so-called realist attitudes of today. The main question is whether these attitudes cost more or less. It is a question we must settle. I think it would be useful to define, in utopian terms, the conditions necessary to bring about the peace of men and nations. Thinking in such terms, provided it is done without fear and without pretensions, can help create the conditions of clear thought and a provisional agreement among men who want to be neither victims nor executioners. In my next articles I shall not attempt to give an absolute answer; I will simply try to correct some of the misconceptions and to pose the question of utopia as accurately as possible. The attempt, in short, is to define the conditions necessary for a political position that is modest—which is to say, free from both messianism and nostalgia for an earthly paradise.

The Confusion of the Socialists

21 November 1946

Once we admit that we have been living in a state of terror for the past ten years, and that terror—no matter how conspicuous or inconspicuous—is the chief source of our anxiety, then we can attempt to see if there is an alternative to terror. This raises the question of European socialism. Terror can be legitimized only if we agree with the principle that the ends justify the means. And this principle can be accepted only if the effectiveness of an action is posed as an absolute end, as in nihilistic ideologies (everything is permitted; what counts is to succeed), or in philosophies that see in history an absolute end (Hegel, followed by Marx, the end being a classless society; everything that leads to it is good).

Such is the problem confronting, for example, the French Socialists. They are bothered by scruples. Once they had only an abstract notion of violence and oppression; now they have seen it firsthand. So they ask themselves whether they too will use such violence, as their philosophy demands, even if only as a temporary expedient and toward a very different end. The author of a recent preface to Saint-Just, speaking of men of an earlier age who had similar scruples, wrote contemptuously: "They recoiled in the face of horrors." Nothing could be truer. And these men have the merit of being despised by all the "strong and superior spirits" who can live among horrors without flinching. At the same time they gave voice to the agonized appeal of common men like ourselves, the millions who make up the raw material of history and who one day must be taken into account despite all contempt.

But our first task is to understand the state of contradiction in which our Socialists now exist. We have not thought enough about the crisis of conscience for French Socialists, as expressed at a recent party congress. It is clear that our Socialists, under the influence of Léon Blum[23] and even more under the pressure of events, have preoccupied themselves to a much greater extent with moral questions (e.g., do the ends justify all the means?) than in the past. They understandably want to base themselves on higher principles than murder. But it is also clear that the same Socialists want to preserve Marxist doctrine. This is because some of them think they cannot be revolutionary without being Marxist, and because others, out of fidelity to party tradition, tell themselves they cannot be Socialist without being

Marxist. The main task of the last party congress was to reconcile the desire for a moral principle that rejects murder with the determination to remain faithful to Marxism. But one cannot reconcile what is irreconcilable.

If it is clear that Marxism is true and that there is logic in history, then political realism is legitimate. It is equally true that if the moral values extolled by the Socialist Party are legitimate, then Marxism is absolutely false, since it claims to be absolutely right. From this point of view, the famous "transcending" Marxism in an idealistic and humanitarian direction is nothing but a joke and an idle dream. It is impossible to "transcend" Marx, for he himself carried his thought to the limits of its consequences. The Communists thus have a logical basis for using the lies and violence that the Socialists reject, yet that basis is the very dialectic which the Socialists want to preserve. It is therefore not surprising that the Socialist congress ended by putting forward two contradictory positions—a conclusion the sterility of which is confirmed by the results of the recent elections.

This way, the confusion will never end. A choice had to be made, but the Socialists would not or could not choose.

My intention is not to chastise the Socialists, but rather to illuminate the paradoxes of our day. To chastise the Socialists, one would have to be superior to them. This is not yet the case. On the contrary, I think this contradiction is true of all those of whom I speak, those who want to be both free and just, but who hesitate before a freedom in which they know justice is finally betrayed, and a justice in which they see freedom suppressed from the start. Those who know "what is to be done" or "what is to be thought" make fun of this intolerable anguish. But I think it would be better, instead of mocking it, to try to understand and clarify this anguish, to see what it means, to explain its near-total condemnation of a world that provokes it, and to extract what little hope there is behind it.

There is indeed hope in this contradiction, for it forces, or will force, the Socialists to make a choice. They will admit that the ends justify the means, which is to say that murder can be legitimized; or they will reject Marxism as an absolute philosophy, confining themselves to its critical aspect, which is often still valuable. If they choose the first, they will end their moral crisis, and their position will be unambiguous. If they choose the second, they will show that our time marks the end of ideologies, that is, absolute utopias which in reality destroy themselves through their enormous costs. Then it will be necessary to choose a new kind of utopia—one that is more modest and less destructive. Thus the refusal to legitimize murder poses the question: what will the Socialists, and what will we, choose?

Yes, that is the question we all must ask; no one, I think, will dare to answer it lightly.

The New Meaning of Revolution

23 November 1946

Since August 1944 everyone has talked about revolution, no doubt with great sincerity. Yet sincerity in itself is not a virtue. There are times when sincerity is so confused that it is worse than lies. The problem of our day is not how to speak with words from the heart, but how to think clearly. Ideally, revolution is a change of political and economic institutions so that freedom and justice can prevail. Realistically, revolution is a complex of often miserable historical events that are meant to bring about this happy transformation.

Can one say that today we use the word "revolution" in its classical sense? When people in France hear talk of revolution, they calmly think of a change in property relations (basically, the private means of production being put under public control), which may be brought about by majority legislation or by a minority coup.

It is easy to see that such thinking has no relevance to contemporary historical circumstances. For one thing, seizing power through violence is a romantic idea; the advanced technology of weapons has made this a fantasy. The oppressive apparatus of the modern state includes the strength of tanks and airplanes, and the only way to fight tanks and airplanes is with tanks and airplanes. 1789 and 1917 are historical dates, but they are no longer historical examples.

But supposing this seizure of power were possible, whether through violence or law, it would be effective only if France (or for that matter Italy or Czechoslovakia) could be put in parentheses and isolated from the rest of the world. For in the current historical situation of 1946, a change in our property system would involve, to give just one example, such consequences for our American credit that the French economy would be threatened with ruin. A revolution from the Right would be no more successful, because of Russia with its million French Communist voters, and because it is the dominant power on the continent. The truth—excuse me for speaking plainly—is that the French are no longer free to make revolution. Or at least, we cannot be revolutionary all by ourselves, since there no longer exists any policy, conservative or Socialist, which can work exclusively within a national framework.

Thus we can speak only of an international revolution. Revolution will take place on an international scale or it will not take place at all. But what meaning does an "international revolution" still hold? There was once a time when it was thought that international reform would be brought about by co-ordinated or simultaneous revolutions—a sort of series of miracles. Today, if our analysis is correct, one can conceive only of the extension of a revolution that has already taken place. This is something that Stalin has understood well, and that is the kindest explanation of his policies (our alternative is to refuse Russia the right of speaking in the name of revolution).

But this reduces us to thinking of Europe and the West as a single nation in which a large, well-armed minority can fight and conquer in order eventually to take control. But if a conservative force (in this case, the United States) is equally well-armed, then clearly the idea of revolution has been replaced by the idea of ideological warfare. More precisely, an international revolution today involves the greatest possible risk of war. Every future revolution will be an imported revolution. It will begin by military occupation—or by the threat of occupation, which is hardly any different. And the revolution will be fulfilled only after the occupying power has conquered the rest of the world.

Revolution has already cost dearly within individual nations. But because of the progress that revolution promises, people have generally accepted the belief that the costs are necessary. Today the cost of another war must be objectively weighed against the progress that one could expect from either Soviet or American world domination. The essential consideration is whether the ends balance the means; for once, let us have enough imagination to see what our world, with its thirty million fresh corpses, would look like after a cataclysm which will cost us ten times as much.

Note that this is a truly objective approach. It takes into account only reality, putting aside for the moment ideological or sentimental considerations. In any case, it must be thought over carefully by all those who speak lightly of revolution. What revolution means *today* must be wholly accepted or wholly rejected.

If one accepts it, one must recognize one's responsibility for the war to come. If one rejects it, one must either declare oneself in favor of the status quo—which is completely utopian, since it assumes that history does not progress—or else find a new definition for the word "revolution," which means assenting to what I call a relative utopia.

After some reflection, I have come to the conclusion that men who want to change the world today must choose one of the following: the charnel house, the impossible dream of stopping history, or the acceptance of a relative utopia which still leaves men the choice to act freely. It is not difficult to see that a relative utopia is the only choice possible, for it is the only choice inspired by reality. In my next article I shall discuss what small chance there is that we shall choose it and thus avoid the charnel house.

International Democracy and Dictatorship

26 November 1946

We know today that there are no more islands and that borders are meaningless. We know that in a world which moves faster and faster, where the Atlantic can be crossed in less than a day and where Moscow can speak to Washington within a matter of hours, we are forced into either fraternity or complicity. The 1940s have taught us that an injury to a student in Prague strikes down simultaneously a worker in Paris, that the blood shed on the banks of a central European river brings a Texas farmer to spill his own blood in the Ardennes, which he sees for the first time. There is no suffering, no torture anywhere in the world which does not affect our everyday lives.

Many Americans would like to continue living closed off in their own society, which they find good. Many Russians would perhaps like to continue their state experiment isolated from the capitalist world. They cannot do so, nor will they ever do so again. Similarly, even the most minor of economic problems cannot be solved outside a community of nations. Europe's bread is in Buenos Aires, Siberian machine tools are made in Detroit. Today tragedy is collective.

We all know, then, beyond the shadow of a doubt, that the new world order we seek can be neither national nor even continental, and certainly not Western or Eastern. It must be universal. We can no longer take hope from partial solutions or concessions. The compromise in which we live means anguish today and murder tomorrow. Meanwhile the pace of history and of the world accelerates. The twenty-one deaf men,[24] the war criminals of tomorrow, talk of peace in monotonous dialogues, while placidly seated in an express train carrying them toward the abyss at a thousand miles per hour. Yes, the question of a world order is the most important question facing us; it must be put ahead of quarrels concerning constitutional and electoral procedure. This problem demands all the resources of our intelligence and willpower.

What are the methods by which we can achieve world unity, by which we can realize this international revolution in which the resources of men, of raw material, of commercial markets and cultural resources will be better distributed?

I see two methods. The first is to unify the world from above, as I wrote yesterday, through a single state more powerful than the others. Both the Russians and the Americans might aspire to such a role. Like many other men I know, I have little with which to answer those who defend the idea that either Russia or America represents ways of controlling and unifying the world according to the ideals of their respective societies. As a Frenchman, and still more as a Mediterranean, I find the idea repugnant. But I will not rely on this sentimental argument. We have but one objection of which I spoke in my last article: unifying the world in such a way would mean war, or at least the extreme risk of war. I will even grant what I do not believe, that this war would not be a nuclear one. But with our present technology, even a conventional war would leave humanity so mutilated and impoverished that the idea of order would be anachronistic. Marx could justify the war of 1870 because it was fought with Chassepot rifles and was limited geographically. In the Marxist perspective, a hundred thousand deaths is a small price to pay for the happiness of hundreds of millions. But today, the certain death of hundreds of millions is no doubt too high a price to pay for the happiness of the few people who might survive. The dizzying rate at which weapons have evolved, a historical fact unforeseen by Marx, forces us to rethink the question of ends and means. In this case, the means would signify the end of the world. No matter what the desired goal, no matter how lofty or necessary it seems, no matter if it promises happiness, justice, and freedom, the means used to reach it represent such an enormous risk and are so greatly disproportionate to the chances of success that we must refuse them.

This brings us to the second method of achieving universal order: the mutual agreement of all parties. The question is not whether this is a possible solution; clearly, it is the only solution. The question is, what exactly does this mean?

The mutual agreement of all parties has a name: international democracy. Of course everyone speaks of the United Nations. But what is international democracy? It is democracy that is international (forgive me this truism, but the most obvious truths are also the most distorted ones). What does democracy, whether national or international, mean? It is a form of society in which law is above the government, in which law is based on the will of all as expressed by a legislative body. And is that what we are to-day trying to achieve? A system of international law is, no doubt, being prepared. But this law can be made or broken by governments, that is, by executive power. We are thus faced with a regime of international dictatorship. The only way to avoid it is to place international law above governments, to put this law in the hands of a parliament, and to determine the parliament through worldwide elections in which all peoples participate. Since we do not have such a parliament, the only way to avoid this international dictatorship is to encourage resistance to it throughout the world and according to means that will not contradict the ends we seek.

The World Goes Fast

27 *November 1946*

It is obvious to everyone that political thought is falling further and further behind events. The French, for example, started the war of 1914 with methods from the war of 1870, and the war of 1939 with the methods of 1918. Of course antiquated thought is not a French specialty. We need only recall that the great powers of today aspire to shape the future with principles developed either in the eighteenth century (liberal capitalism) or in the nineteenth (so-called "scientific" socialism). These systems of thought which, in the first case, date from the first years of modern industrialism, and in the second, from the age of Darwinism and Renanian optimism, now try to take on the age of the atom bomb, sudden mutations, and nihilism. What could better illustrate the increasing and increasingly dangerous divergence of political thought from historical reality?

It is true that consciousness is always somewhat behind reality; history rushes forward while thought reflects. But the inevitable discrepancy becomes greater as history moves faster and faster. The world has changed far more in the past fifty years than it did in the preceding two centuries. Thus we see nations quarreling over borders, when we all know that borders have become abstractions. It was nationalism that seemed to prevail at the Conference of the 21.

This is what must be avoided as we try to analyze our historical reality. We should not be concentrating our political thinking on the German problem, which is a secondary problem compared to the clash of empires that threatens us. But if tomorrow we resolve the Russo-American conflict, we may still find ourselves outdistanced. The clash of empires is already becoming secondary to the clash of civilizations. Everywhere the colonial peoples are demanding that their voices be heard. Perhaps in ten years, perhaps in fifty, the pre-eminence of Western civilization will be in question. We might as well recognize this now and admit these civilizations into the world parliament, so that its laws will be truly universal and a universal order will be established.

The veto issue in the U.N. today is a false issue, because the conflicting minorities and majorities are false. The U.S.S.R. will always have the right to refuse majority rule as long as it is a majority of ministers and not a majority of peoples represented by their delegates. The day when that majority comes into being, all must obey it, all must accept the will of the majority.

Similarly, if we constantly keep in mind that the pace of our lives *is* accelerating, then perhaps we can understand our economic problems. In 1930 the question of socialism was not the same as in 1848. Collectivization of the modes of production was a logical extension of the idea that ownership must be abolished. But collectivization was conceived not only in order to abolish ownership, but also to deal with the enlarged scale of the economy. But since 1930 the scale of the economy has grown again. Just as the political solution must be an international one, so the economic solution must be directed at the means of international production: petroleum, coal, and uranium. If we must have collectivization, it should start with resources that are indispensable to everyone and which are, in truth, owned by no one. As for the rest—that will be decided by electoral discourse.

These ideas perhaps seem utopian to some; but for all who refuse to accept the risks of war, they must be resolutely affirmed and defended. And we cannot imagine putting these ideas into practice without the help of former Socialists and all the other isolated progressivists throughout the world today.

In any case, I shall reply once more and finally to the accusations of utopia. For us the choice is simple: utopia or a war that has been prepared for by outdated modes of thought. The world must choose today between either antiquated political thought or utopian thought. Antiquated thought is killing us. As skeptical as we are (myself included), realism forces us to choose this relative utopia. Once our utopia has become a part of history, then, as with so many other utopias of its kind, men will not be able to conceive of reality without it. For history is nothing but the desperate efforts of men to give truth to their most clairvoyant dreams.

A New Social Contract

29 November 1946

It all comes down to this: the fate of men of all nations will be uncertain, until we have settled the problems of peace and world order. There will be no successful revolution anywhere in the world until *this* revolution has been completed. All those in France who today say otherwise speak either in vain or out of self-interest. I will go even further. Not only will there be no change in property relations anywhere in the world, but even the simplest problems—how to provide bread everyday to end the hunger from which all Europe suffers, or how to provide enough coal to keep our society running—will not be solved until we have peace.

Each form of contemporary political thought which refuses to justify lies and murder, no matter how realistic or unrealistic it may otherwise be, will be led to this conclusion and must accept it calmly and with reason. It must also accept the following points: (1) that domestic policy is in itself a secondary matter; (2) that the main problem is the creation of a world order that will bring us the lasting structural reforms which are the true mark of revolution; and (3) that within any given nation there exist now only administrative problems, to be solved provisionally and as well as possible while awaiting a solution that is more effective because more universal.

The French constitution, for example, can be judged only on the basis of whether or not it supports a world order founded on justice and dialogue. From this point of view, we must condemn our constitution's indifference to even the most basic human rights. We must also recognize that the problem of restoring the food supply is ten times more important than the problems of nationalization or election figures. Nationalization will no longer be viable if carried out only by an individual country. And while the food supply is another task that cannot be addressed on only the national level, it is a pressing enough problem to demand at least temporary domestic solutions.

The consequence of all this is that we now have a criterion for judging domestic policy that we lacked before. The editorialists of *Aube* and *Humanité*[25] can contradict each other as much as they like, but that will not make us forget that both newspapers, together with the parties they represent, acquiesced in the annexation without referendum of Briga and Tenda,[26] and that they are thus accomplices in the destruction of international democracy. M. Bidault and M. Thorez,[27] no matter how good their intentions, both favor the principles of international dictatorship. From this point of view, despite whatever one thinks of them, they represent in our politics not realism but the most disastrous kind of utopia.

Yes, we must stop thinking only of domestic problems. One cannot end a plague with the same remedies used for a headache. A crisis that tears the whole world apart must be met on a world scale. Order for all, so that the weight of misery and fear will be lessened for each, is our logical objective today. But that calls for action and sacrifices, that is, for human beings. And if there are many today who within their hearts detest violence and killing, there are not many who are willing to reconsider their actions and thoughts. For those who do make this effort, however, in so doing they will find a reasonable hope and the habit of action.

They will admit that they do not expect much from their current governments, for these live and act according to murderous principles. The only hope resides in what is most difficult, which is to begin things anew, to build a society that will live within the shell of a society that has been condemned. Men must therefore, as individuals, create among themselves, both within and across borders, a new social contract which will unite men according to more reasonable principles.

The movement toward peace of which I speak could start within nations as work communities, and internationally as intellectual communities; the former, organized co-operatively, would help as many individuals as possible with their material needs, while the latter would try to define the values by which this international community would live, and also plead its cause on every occasion.

More precisely, the latter's task would be to oppose the confusion of terror with clear language, while at the same time defining the values which are indispensable to a peaceful world. Their first objective could be the creation of a code of international justice whose first article would be the abolition of the death penalty, and a declaration of the principles necessary for a civilization in which men speak and listen to one another. Such work would answer the needs of an age which finds itself with no philosophical justification for the thirst for brotherhood which today burns in Western man. It is not, of course, a matter of constructing a new ideology, but simply of pursuing a certain style of life.

In any case, these are only some of the motives for reflection, which are too numerous to enumerate in the short space of these articles. But to return to more concrete terms: let us suppose that certain men resolve that they will consistently oppose power with force of example, domination with exhortation, insult with dialogue, and trickery with simple honor. Let us suppose that they refuse all the advantages of contemporary society and accept only the duties and responsibilities that bind them to other men. Let us suppose that they devote themselves to orienting education, the press, and public opinion toward the principles of conduct as outlined here. Then I say that these men will not be acting out of hopes for utopia, but out of honest realism. They will be preparing for the future by knocking down some of the walls that keep us from it. If realism is the art of taking into account both present and future, of obtaining the most while sacrificing the least, then who could fail to see the glaring realism of their behavior?

Whether or not these men will arise, I do not know. It is probable that most of them are at this moment thinking things over, and that is good. But it is certain that the effectiveness of their action cannot be separated from the courage with which they will renounce certain dreams, so as to cling only to what saves lives. Once they have chosen, it will perhaps be necessary for them, before they are done, to raise their voices.

Toward Dialogue

30 November 1946

Yes, we must raise our voices. Up to this point, I have refrained from appealing to the forces of emotion. Today we are being torn apart by the "logic of history," which exists not in history but only in our minds, but which nonetheless threatens to destroy us. It is not emotion that can cut the knots of this irrational "logic," but reason itself, along with the true logic that works within reason's boundaries. But I would not want to finish by leaving the impression that our hopes for the future can be achieved without the force of our indignation and love. I know well that it takes powerful motives to drive men to action, to make them accept a struggle whose objectives are so limited and whose chances for success are so small. Still, this is not a question of inciting men to be carried away by emotion. On the contrary, it is essential that they not be carried away, that they understand clearly what they are doing.

To save what can be saved and leave ourselves a chance for the future—that is our motive and logic, our passion and sacrifice. We ask only that men think it over carefully and then decide whether they will add to the misery of the world to achieve vague and distant goals, and whether they will accept a world crowded with weapons where brother kills brother; or whether, on the contrary, they will avoid as much bloodshed as possible in order to give future generations—who will be even better armed than ourselves—a chance for survival.

For my part, I am quite sure that I have made the choice. And having chosen, I think that I must speak, that I must say that I will never again be among those who, for whatever reasons, accommodate themselves to murder, and that I accept the consequences of my choice. The task is done, and this is as far as I can go at present. But before concluding, I want to make clear the spirit in which these articles are written.

We are asked to love or hate such and such a country and such and such a people. But we are among those who feel too strongly our common bonds with all men to make such a choice. Those who really care about the Russian people, who recognize what they have always been—that leavening world of which Tolstoy and Gorky speak—do not wish them success in their power politics, but rather want to spare them, after so many past ordeals, new and even greater bloodshed. The same is true for the American people and for all the peoples of unhappy Europe. This is the kind of elementary truth that one forgets amid the furious passions of our time.

Yes, what we must fight is fear and silence, and with them the spiritual isolation they involve. What we must defend is dialogue and the universal communication of men. Slavery, injustice, and lies are the plagues that destroy this dialogue and forbid this communication, and that is why we must reject them. But today these plagues are the very substance of history, hence many consider them necessary evils. It is true that we cannot escape history, for we are in it up to our necks. But one can attempt to fight within history to keep a certain part of ourselves out of history. That is all I have wanted to say here. And yet, I feel the need to go still further in clarifying the attitude and spirit in which I have tried to write these articles; I want to make sure, before closing, that the reader will hear me in good faith.

All the nations of the world today are involved in an enormous experiment which works according to the laws of power and domination. I will not say whether or not we should try to hinder their experiment. They hardly seem to want our help, and for the moment they laugh at our attempts to interfere with them. The experiment, then, will continue. But let me ask a simple question. What if the experiment fails, what if the logic of history, on which so many lives depend, turns out to be wrong? What if, despite two or three world wars, despite the sacrifices of several generations and a whole system of values, our grandchildren—supposing they survive—find themselves no closer to a world society? It may be that the survivors of this experiment will be too weak to understand their own agony. But since it is inevitable that the experiment will go on, it is good that some men have accepted the task of preserving, through the apocalyptic history that awaits us, the modest thoughtfulness which, without pretending to solve everything, will always be ready to give human meaning to everyday life. The essential thing is that these men weigh carefully, and once and for all, the price they have to pay.

To conclude: for the moment, all I can ask in the midst of a murderous world is that we agree to reflect on murder and to make a choice. If this can be done, we will be divided into those who accept murder as a last resort, and those who refuse murder no matter what. Since this terrifying dividing line actually exists, it will mark progress if we can at least make it clear. In the coming years an endless struggle will be waged across five continents, a struggle in which either violence or dialogue will prevail. Granted, the former has a thousand times the chances of the latter. But I have always thought that if the man who places hope in the human condition is a fool, then he who gives up hope in the face of circumstances is a coward. Henceforth, the only honor will lie in obstinately holding to a formidable gamble: that words are stronger than bullets.

Conclusion

CAMUS'S RESIGNATION
FROM *COMBAT*

To Our Readers

3 June 1947

The editorial and administrative staff of *Combat* today re-
sign their positions as directors of this paper, although *Combat*
itself will continue to appear daily. This of course demands an
explanation, which I will try to give here as clearly as possible.

Combat today has a large number of readers, which for a newspaper without financial ambition should be enough to assure its
continued existence. But in truth, the conditions of running a
daily paper are such that only papers with huge circulations can
ever break even. I leave it to the reader's imagination to decide
what this simple rule of economics means for freedom of the press.

Even though *Combat* is currently running a deficit, it had
earned enough money in the past so that we thought we could
wait a while before trying to increase circulation through new
organization and through greater appeals to our loyal readers.
That would have been possible, had not the printers' strike taken
away the few million francs we had saved, the product of relentless work by all of *Combat*'s staff.

Of course we could have asked for money from the outside; indeed, we could have received money without even asking for it.

We were made a number of offers, many of which were both generous and honorable. However, given our strong feeling that a newspaper must be independent, we did not accept these offers. During recent weeks the *Combat* team has fought alone and with diminished means to save the paper and to keep our personnel from unemployment. It would not have been possible to come this far without the greatest efforts from all our staff. But finally we realized the need for change, and that our tenure as directors of this paper had come to an end.

We do not have exclusive ownership of the title *Combat*. The paper belongs morally and legally to all those who during the Occupation wrote, printed, and distributed it. We are therefore very glad to be able to return the paper to one of the original members of the Combat movement. After consultation with the Federation of Combat Veterans, it has been decided that our comrade Claude Bourdet, one of the founders of the underground *Combat,* who was arrested and deported during the Occupation, and whose political leanings have always been very close to our own, will take charge of the management of this paper. . . .

And so our political and administrative direction of this paper has ended and gives way to new direction. This must be clear. We have the sincerest wishes for the success of an enterprise that has been so dear to us. But just as our comrades will not be responsible for the decisions we made, so our departure releases us from responsibility for their actions. It is understood, of course, that Claude Bourdet has every intention of continuing this paper with the traditional objectivity and independence that have become its trademark. In nearly every respect, the running of this paper will remain the same.

It remains only to thank our readers for the confidence and loyalty they have always shown us. There are several ways to make one's fortune in journalism. I need not say that *Combat* is not one of them! But the true reward was the respect we had for our readers. And if it so happens that, from time to time, the respect was returned, then that was luxury! Of course we made some mistakes (but then, who did not?). But we never relinquished any of the honor that goes with our profession.

It is true that this is not a paper like the others; that has always been our pride. Perhaps that is the best way to describe, without immodesty, the feeling we have as we leave *Combat* today.

NOTES
SELECTED BIBLIOGRAPHY
INDEX

Notes

Introduction

1. Marie Granet and Henri Michel, *Combat* (Paris: Presses Universitaires de France, 1957), p. 136.
2. Emmett Parker, *Albert Camus: The Artist in the Arena* (Madison: University of Wisconsin Press, 1966), p. 61.
3. Susan Tarrow, *Exile from the Kingdom: A Political Rereading of Albert Camus* (University, Ala.: University of Alabama Press, 1985), p. 101.
4. Herbert R. Lottman, *Albert Camus: A Biography* (New York: Doubleday and Company, 1979), p. 341.
5. Fred H. Willhoite, Jr., *Beyond Nihilism: Albert Camus's Contribution to Political Thought* (Baton Rouge: Louisiana State University Press, 1968), p. 54.
6. Tarrow, p. 32.
7. *Alger-Républicain*, 3 December 1938, p. 1. Quoted by Parker, p. 18.
8. Lottman, p. 148.
9. Patrick McCarthy, *Camus* (New York: Random House, 1982), p. 77.
10. Albert Camus, *Carnets, 1935–1942* (Paris: Gallimard, 1962), p. 29.
11. Lottman, p. 149.
12. Lottman, p. 153.
13. Albert Camus and Jean Grenier, *Correspondance, 1932–1960* (Paris: Gallimard, 1981), p. 31.
14. *Carnets, 1935–1942*, p. 99.
15. Parker, p. 21.
16. Parker, p. 22.

17. Lottman speculates that El Okbi may have actually been guilty. See Lottman, pp. 196–98, for a more thorough discussion of this complex affair.
18. Parker, p. 48.
19. McCarthy, p. 125.
20. Lottman, p. 209.
21. *Soir-Républicain*, 9 September 1939, p. 1. Quoted by Parker, p. 49.
22. McCarthy, p. 126.
23. *Carnets, 1935–1942*, p. 203.
24. Albert Ollivier, "Albert Camus et le refus de l'éternel," *L'Arche* (October–November 1944), p. 159. Quoted by Willhoite, p. 42.
25. Willhoite, p. 39.
26. Tarrow, p. 74.
27. Albert Camus, *L'Etranger* (Paris: Gallimard, 1942), p. 157.
28. John Cruickshank, *Albert Camus and the Literature of Revolt* (New York: Oxford University Press, 1959), p. 58.
29. Cruickshank, p. 86.
30. Parker, p. 71.
31. Albert Camus, *Carnets, 1942–1951* (Paris: Gallimard, 1964), p. 53.
32. Tarrow, p. 94.
33. See, for example, Parker, pp. 60–61.
34. Granet and Michel, p. 145.
35. *Revue libre*, no. 2, 1943; *Cahiers de la libération*, no. 3, 1944. The third and fourth letters were written for *Revue libre* but did not appear until the letters were published together in *Lettres à un ami allemand* (Paris: Gallimard, 1945).
36. Albert Camus, *Resistance, Rebellion and Death*, translated by Justin O'Brien (New York: Alfred A. Knopf, 1960), p. 27.
37. *Resistance, Rebellion and Death*, pp. 27–28.
38. *Resistance, Rebellion and Death*, p. 28.
39. See Robert Aron, *France Reborn*, translated by Humphrey Hare (New York: Charles Scribner's Sons, 1964), pp. 240 ff.; and Alexander Werth, *France: 1940–1955* (New York: Henry Holt and Company, 1956), p. 217.
40. Werth, p. 216.
41. Werth, p. 136.
42. "Manifeste des M.U.R.," *Combat clandestin*, no. 34 (September 1942), p. 1. Quoted by Parker, p. 57.
43. Parker, p. 75. See also the outline of the Comité National de la Résistance (C.N.R.) charter given by Werth, pp. 222–23.
44. Parker, p. 83.

45. Werth, pp. 227–28.
46. Werth, p. 239.
47. Parker, p. 91.
48. Werth, p. 285.
49. Lottman, p. 349.
50. Parker, p. 113.
51. Albert Camus, *Actuelles I* (Paris: Gallimard, 1950), p. 172.
52. Albert Camus, *The Rebel*, translated by Anthony Bower (New York: Alfred A. Knopf, 1956; Vintage Books, 1972), p. 293.
53. *The Rebel*, pp. 281, 310.
54. McCarthy, p. 236.
55. Bernard Murchland, "The Anatomy of a Quarrel," in the appendix to *Choice of Action* by Michel-Antoine Burnier, translated by Bernard Murchland (New York: Random House, 1968), p. 179.
56. Murchland, p. 179.
57. Jean-Paul Sartre, "Reply to Albert Camus," in *Situations*, translated by Benita Eisler (New York: George Braziller, 1965), pp. 72, 73, 104. Quoted by Murchland, pp. 184–88.
58. Willhoite, p. 162.
59. Tarrow, p. 194.
60. Willhoite, p. 160.
61. Albert Camus, *Actuelles III* (Paris: Gallimard, 1958), p. 28. Quoted by Parker, p. 167.
62. Willhoite, p. 162.
63. Albert Camus, *Essais* (Paris: Gallimard, 1965), p. 974. Quoted by Tarrow, p. 196.
64. Parker, pp. 165–66.
65. Parker, p. 166.
66. Albert Camus, *Notebooks, 1942–1951*, translated by Philip Thody (New York: Alfred A. Knopf, 1966), p. 215. Quoted by Willhoite, p. 143.
67. *Essais*, p. 1072. Quoted by Tarrow, p. 199.

Text

1. The Forces Françaises de l'Intérieur (F.F.I.), sometimes called the French Secret Army, was basically an amalgam of all French Resistance groups, which Jean Moulin placed under the command of General Dalestraint at the beginning of 1943. By 1944 the F.F.I. included units large enough to conduct open battles with German troops and play a significant role in the liberation of France.

2. Henri-Philippe Pétain (1856–1951), marshal of France, had become a national hero for his victory at the battle of Verdun in 1916. After the German attack of May 1940, Paul Reynaud, then head of government, named Pétain vice premier; at the fall of France in June, Pétain was asked to form a new government. The Assembly conferred almost absolute powers on him. But in 1942, after all France had been occupied, the Germans transferred his powers to Laval, though Pétain stayed on as a figurehead. He was taken to Germany by force in 1944. He was returned to France and sentenced to death in 1945, but his sentence was immediately commuted to life imprisonment.

3. See Introduction, p. 19.

4. "[O]ne of the greatest among us" certainly refers to André Malraux, whose novel *The Age of Scorn* (*Le Temps du mépris*) had been adapted for the stage by Camus in 1936.

5. Camille Chautemps (1885–1963) held numerous ministries from 1924 to 1940. As a cabinet member in 1940, he was one of the first to suggest surrender to the Germans and was among the architects of the Armistice. He briefly held a portfolio in the Pétain government but left France in 1940 for the United States, where he spent the rest of his life.

  Albert Chichery (1888–1944), a rather minor political figure compared to Chautemps, was minister of commerce and industry under Paul Reynaud. In 1940 he voted to turn constitutional powers over to Pétain and was subsequently made a member of the National Council created by the Vichy government. At the Liberation, on 15 August 1944, a group of unknown men kidnapped him from his home at Madrolles, took him to a nearby woods, and shot him to death. No one ever learned who the men were.

6. Marcel Petiot, a serial killer, received considerable attention in the French press. A middle-aged medical doctor, he was dubbed the "modern Bluebeard" after remains of some of his forty-odd victims were discovered in his basement.

7. The Mouvement de Libération Nationale (M.L.N.) was a chiefly non-Communist Resistance organization formed after the Liberation. It sought to make itself a political party but was too disorganized and strife-torn to do so.

8. "I prefer injustice to disorder." Goethe, *The Siege of Mainz*.

9. Daniel Mayer (b. 1909) was secretary-general of the Socialist Party, 1943–46, and had been editor-in-chief of the underground Resistance paper *Le Populaire*.

Félix Gouin (1884–1977) was a prominent Socialist, head of the Consultative Assembly in Algeria and then in Paris, and head of the provisional government from January to June 1946.

10. Metz, near the border of Germany, was liberated by Patton's Third Army between 19 and 21 November 1944.

11. Jules Guesde was the pseudonym of Mathieu Basile (1845–1922), an organizer and early leader of the French labor movement.

12. Camus's editorial of 30 November 1944 denounced the government's plan to reduce the number of newspaper copies printed in Paris by 25 percent as an attempt "to deprive the Resistance of its means of expression." Camus suggested that the government was motivated "by interests hostile to the Resistance and to reform" and added that, in France and throughout the rest of Europe, an offensive against the Resistance had begun.

13. Edgar Quinet (1805–75), poet, historian, and political philosopher, was author of, among other works, *La Révolution* (1865). Quinet had originally hailed the revolution of February 1848, but after Louis-Napoléon's coup d'état of December 1851 he was forced to leave France.

14. Georges Bernanos (1888–1948), novelist and essayist, was one of the most original and independent Catholic writers of his time. He was the author of, among other political pamphlets, *A Diary of My Times* (1938), a fierce polemic against the fascist excesses of the Spanish Civil War and the Church dignitaries who supported them.

15. René Leynaud was a poet whom Camus had met in Lyons in 1942, and to whom Camus had taken an instant liking. Leynaud may well have been one of Camus's first contacts with the Combat organization. Arrested by Vichy in May 1944, Leynaud was shot in the legs as he tried to escape. Taken prisoner, he was executed by the Germans as they prepared to leave the city.

"Vélin" was the pseudonym of André Bollier, who had been in charge of printing and distributing the underground *Combat*. In March 1944 he had been arrested by the Gestapo and tortured, but he did not talk and was subsequently released. He was killed in June 1944 in a shootout with the police.

16. Henri Béraud was a writer and critic for *Gringoire*, an ultrarightist but anti-German weekly. He was tried and sentenced to death in January 1945, but de Gaulle commuted his sentence to life imprisonment. He was released from prison in 1950.

17. Marcel Cachin (1869–1958) was a veteran Communist and the senior deputy in the Assembly from 1946 to 1951.

18. Hitler committed suicide on 30 April 1945; on 8 May the surrender of all German forces was signed.
19. The atomic bomb was dropped on Hiroshima on 6 August 1945.
20. The L.V.F., or Légion des Volontaires Français, was a French legion fighting for the Germans on the Russian Front.
21. *L'Oeuvre* was the pro-Nazi newspaper of which Marcel Déat, one of the most fervent and well-known French Nazis, was an editor.
22. Gérin's sentence was eventually commuted and he was released in October 1946. He recovered his rights and worked as a journalist for *Le Figaro*.
23. Léon Blum (1872–1950) was the first Socialist—and the first Jewish—prime minister of France. He was twice premier during the 1930s. He was arrested by Vichy in 1942 and spent the rest of the war in prison, but contributed to the Resistance through his correspondence. After the Liberation, Blum served as a special ambassador to the United States. From December 1946 to January 1947 he presided over the provisional government.
24. Representatives of twenty-one of the Allied nations had convened at the Paris Peace Conference on 29 July 1946 to decide the fate of Germany's European allies, Italy, Rumania, Hungary, Bulgaria, and Finland. Camus refers later, in "The World Goes Fast," to the "Conference of the 21."
25. *Aube* and *Humanité* were the newspapers of the Christian Democratic Party and the Communist Party, respectively.
26. Briga and Tenda are towns along the Franco-Italian border. Possession of the towns was disputed by France and Italy after the war.
27. Georges Bidault (1899–1983) was a member of the Christian Democratic Party. He was head of the National Council of Resistance in 1943, foreign minister in de Gaulle's provisional government in 1945, head of the provisional government in 1946, and foreign minister again in 1947–48.

   Maurice Thorez (1900–66) was a prominent Communist who served as a minister of state in de Gaulle's provisional government in 1945, and was a vice premier in 1947. He was head of the French Communist Party in the 1950s.

Selected Bibliography

Works by Albert Camus

Actuelles I: Chroniques 1944–1948. Paris: Gallimard, 1950.
Actuelles II: Chroniques 1948–1953. Paris: Gallimard, 1953.
Actuelles III: Chroniques algériennes. Paris: Gallimard, 1958.
Le Combat d'Albert Camus. Articles selected and annotated, with an introduction, by Norman Stokle. Quebec: Les Presses de l'Université Laval, 1970.
Correspondance, 1932–1960. Albert Camus and Jean Grenier. Edited by Marguerite Dobrenn. Paris: Gallimard, 1981.
Essais. Edited by R. Quillot and L. Faucon, with a critical introduction by R. Quillot. Paris: Gallimard, 1965.
Fragments d'un combat, 1938–1940: Alger-Républicain, le Soir-Républicain. Edited by Jacqueline Lévi-Valensi and André Abbou. Paris: Gallimard, 1978.
"Lettre au Directeur des *Temps modernes*." *Les Temps modernes,* no. 82 (August 1952), pp. 323–33.
Lettres à un ami allemand. Paris: Gallimard, 1945.
The Myth of Sisyphus. Translated by Justin O'Brien. New York: Alfred A. Knopf, 1955. Originally published as *Le Mythe de Sisyphe,* Paris: Gallimard, 1942.
"Neither Victims nor Executioners." Translated by Dwight Macdonald. *Politics,* vol. 4, no. 4 (July–August 1947), 141–47.
Notebooks: 1935–1942. Translated by Philip Thody. New York: Alfred A. Knopf, 1963. Originally published as *Carnets: 1935–1942,* Paris: Gallimard, 1962.

Selected Bibliography

Notebooks: 1942–1951. Translated by Philip Thody. New York: Alfred A. Knopf, 1966. Originally published as Carnets: 1942–1951, Paris: Gallimard, 1964.
The Plague. Translated by Stuart Gilbert. New York: Alfred A. Knopf, 1948. Originally published as La Peste, Paris: Gallimard, 1947.
The Rebel. Translated by Anthony Bower. New York: Alfred A. Knopf, 1956; Vintage Books, 1972. Originally published as L'Homme révolté, Paris: Gallimard, 1951.
Resistance, Rebellion and Death. Translated by Justin O'Brien. New York: Alfred A. Knopf, 1961.
The Stranger. Translated by Stuart Gilbert. New York: Alfred A. Knopf, 1946. Originally published as L'Etranger, Paris: Gallimard, 1942.

Other Works

Aron, Robert. France Reborn. Translated by Humphrey Hare. New York: Charles Scribner's Sons, 1964.
Barthes, Roland. "La Peste, annales d'une épidémie ou roman de la solitude." Club, February 1955, p. 6.
Bieber, Konrad. L'Allemagne vue par les écrivains de la Résistance française, with a preface by Albert Camus. Geneva: Droz, 1954.
Brée, Germaine. Camus, rev. ed. New Brunswick: Rutgers University Press, 1961.
Cruickshank, John. Albert Camus and the Literature of Revolt. New York: Oxford University Press, 1959.
Doubrovsky, Serge. "The Ethics of Albert Camus." In Camus: A Collection of Critical Essays, edited by Germaine Brée, pp. 71–84. Englewood Cliffs, N.J.: Prentice-Hall, 1962.
Granet, Marie, and Michel, Henri. Combat. Paris: Presses Universitaires de France, 1957.
Grenier, Jean. Albert Camus: Souvenirs. Paris: Gallimard, 1968.
Lottman, Herbert R. Albert Camus: A Biography. New York: Doubleday and Company, 1979.
McCarthy, Patrick. Camus: A Critical Study of His Life and Work. London: Hamish Hamilton, 1982.
Mauriac, Francois. "Lettre III: Réponse à Albert Camus." La Table ronde, no. 14 (February 1949), pp. 199–206.
———. "Le Mépris de la charité." Le Figaro, no. 122 (7–8 January 1945), p. 1.
———. "Réponse à Combat." Le Figaro, no. 55 (22–23 October 1944), p. 1.

———. "La Vocation de la Résistance." *Le Figaro,* no. 91 (3–4 December 1944), p. 1.

Michel, Henri. *Histoire de la Résistance.* Paris: Presses Universitaires de France, 1950.

Murchland, Bernard. "Sartre and Camus: The Anatomy of a Quarrel." In Michel-Antoine Burnier, *Choice of Action,* translated by Bernard Murchland. New York: Random House, 1968.

O'Brien, Connor Cruise. *Albert Camus of Europe and Africa.* New York: Viking Press, 1970.

Ollivier, Albert. "Albert Camus et le refus de l'éternel." *L'Arche,* October–November 1944.

Parker, Emmett. *Albert Camus: The Artist in the Arena.* Madison: University of Wisconsin Press, 1966.

Quilliot, Roger. *The Sea and Prisons: A Commentary on the Life and Thought of Albert Camus.* Translated by Emmett Parker. University, Ala.: University of Alabama Press, 1970.

Sartre, Jean-Paul. "Réponse à Albert Camus." *Les Temps modernes,* no. 82 (August 1952), pp. 334–53.

———. *Situations.* Translated by Benita Eisler. New York: George Braziller, 1965.

Tarrow, Susan. *Exile from the Kingdom: A Political Rereading of Albert Camus.* University, Ala.: University of Alabama Press, 1985.

Thody, Philip. *Albert Camus: A Study of His Work.* New York: Grove Press, 1959.

———. *Albert Camus: 1913–1960.* New York: Macmillan, 1962.

Werth, Alexander. *France, 1940–1955.* New York: Henry Holt and Company, 1956.

Willhoite, Fred H., Jr. *Beyond Nihilism: Albert Camus's Contribution to Political Thought.* Baton Rouge: Louisiana State University Press, 1968.

Index

Index

Index

Index

Index

UNIVERSITY PRESS OF NEW ENGLAND publishes books under its own imprint and is the publisher for Brandeis University Press, Brown University Press, Clark University Press, University of Connecticut, Dartmouth College, Middlebury College Press, University of New Hampshire, University of Rhode Island, Tufts University, University of Vermont, and Wesleyan University Press.

ABOUT THE TRANSLATOR

Alexandre de Gramont's grandfather was killed in 1944 flying a bomber for the RAF; he had sent his family to safety after joining de Gaulle and the free French in England at the outbreak of the war. De Gramont was the first member of his family to be born in America. He compiled and translated this book while an undergraduate at Wesleyan University, from which he received a B.A. in 1986. He received his J.D. from New York University School of Law in 1990, following which he served as a law clerk to Justice Alan B. Handler of the Supreme Court of New Jersey. He now practices law in Washington, D.C.

ABOUT THE BOOK

Between Hell and Reason was composed on a Mergenthaler 202 in Sabon, a contemporary typeface designed by the late Swiss typographer, teacher, scholar, book designer, and type designer Jan Tschichold. The book was composed by G & S Typesetters, Inc. of Austin, Texas, and designed by Kachergis Book Design of Pittsboro, North Carolina.